Flavor

Flavor

SABRINA GHAYOUR

ASTER*

For Connor and Olly . . .
. . . who have both taught me more about food and life than they'll ever know.
I'm so happy that you've become more adventurous eaters and I'm very proud
of you both. Here's to many, many adventures ahead!

ASTER

First published in Great Britain in 2023
by Aster, an imprint of
Octopus Publishing Group Ltd
Carmelite House
50 Victoria Embankment
London EC4Y 0DZ
www.octopusbooks.co.uk

An Hachette UK Company
www.hachette.co.uk

Text copyright © Sabrina Ghayour 2023
Photography copyright © Kris Kirkham 2023
Design and layout copyright © Octopus
Publishing Group 2023

Distributed in the US by
Hachette Book Group
1290 Avenue of the Americas
4th and 5th Floors, New York, NY 10104

Distributed in Canada by
Canadian Manda Group
664 Annette St.
Toronto, Ontario, Canada M6S 2C8

Sabrina Ghayour asserts her moral right
to be identified as the author of this work.

ISBN 978 1 78325 595 5
Printed and bound in China

10 9 8 7 6 5 4 3 2 1

Publisher: Stephanie Jackson
Senior Managing Editor: Sybella Stephens
Copy Editor: Jo Richardson
Art Director: Jaz Bahra
Photographer: Kris Kirkham
Food Stylist: Laura Field
Props Stylist: Agathe Gits
Senior Production Manager: Peter Hunt

Author's notes
Sabrina uses level measuring spoons unless
specified otherwise.
Look for the V symbol on cheese and
wine vinegars to ensure they are suitable
for vegans.

FSC
www.fsc.org
MIX
Paper | Supporting
responsible forestry
FSC® C008047

Contents

INTRODUCTION 6

SALADS 9

LITTLE BITES & SAVORY TREATS 49

MEAT, POULTRY, FISH & SEAFOOD 89

VEGETABLES & LEGUMES 137

PASTA, NOODLES & GRAINS 187

SWEET 217

INDEX 236

ACKNOWLEDGMENTS 240

Introduction

The more books I write, the more I learn about what truly matters versus what doesn't when cooking. One thing I have learned is that when all is said and done, no matter who we are, we all face very similar challenges at home when it comes to cooking. We are often time-poor and not always able to plan ahead. Sometimes we don't have the right ingredients on hand and, more often these days, cost is an increasingly worrying factor.

Three words rule the recipes I like to write: simple, flavorful, and economical. And in order to stick to these principles, I choose to write the kind of recipes that remain straightforward, accessible, adaptable, and always full of flavor.

Flavor is such an important element of my cooking. No matter what food I make, or where or what I eat, taste is everything. To me, flavor is comfort, satisfaction, and even nostalgia, but importantly, it never has to be complicated, heavy-handed, or extreme. Life is too short to eat bland food! Sometimes a little seasoning, a flourish of herbs, a squeeze of lemon, or a drizzle of honey is all it takes to really elevate an otherwise simple dish into something that suddenly bursts with big, bold flavor. I get so much pleasure from the simplest of flavors that sometimes I wonder if all I need is salt and pepper to carry me through life. However, I have so much appreciation for a well stocked kitchen cupboard, and for me, opening the door of my cupboard can create a myriad of new possibilities, delivering endless combinations for vibrant and exciting new tastes using ingredients that you may also have tucked away in your cupboard.

By far the biggest lesson I have learned when it comes to cooking and writing recipes is that it takes a degree of bravery to keep things simple. Less is almost always more, and this is never a bad thing. In fact, almost a decade after my first book, *Persiana*, I can confirm that it is possibly one of the reasons my readers embrace my books and recipes as much as they do.

So, this book, lucky number 7, has been written to be full of flavor in the simplest and most pared-back way I know. Many dishes are perfect for quick midweek meals, and others you may prefer to make when you have a little more time on your hands, but as always, you can easily swap or substitute ingredients if you need to, using up whatever you have at home or better suits your tastes. Rest assured that if an ingredient or method must be adhered to then I will always stress this in the recipe. So feel free to use these recipes as a great base for creating simple but vibrant meals in your own home. Nothing gives me greater joy than to hear when readers have embraced my recipes, and I love to learn about how dishes have evolved in different households when they have been made time and time again.

Whatever you like to eat and however much time and budget you have, there is plenty on offer for everyone in this book and almost everything can be adapted to suit every taste. So, what are you waiting for? Dive in and explore this collection of colorful new recipes, that are, simply put, full of flavor!

Sabrina Ghayour

Salads

Aegean Giant Couscous Salad

For me, a salad has to pack in some big flavors, especially when using grains. I like mine to be savory, sometimes sweet, sharp, refreshing, crunchy, and aromatic, and for each mouthful to be a little well seasoned flavor bomb that will make me want to eat more and more. The Turks have a word for recipes that have a slightly Aegean vibe—*ege* (pronounced eg-eh)—and if this wasn't my own creation, it would very much be an *ege salatasi*. This is sunshine and all its flavors packed into a salad. This is vacations in Turkey and Greece served on a plate . . . zingy, herby, crunchy, and satisfying. I absolutely love this dish and serve it on repeat throughout the summer because it's a real crowd-pleaser.

SERVES 6 TO 8

9oz giant couscous

14oz can chickpeas, drained

10½oz semi-dried tomatoes in oil, drained and cut into strips

9oz block of halloumi cheese, grated

3 handfuls of pitted Kalamata olives

1 red bell pepper, cored, seeded, and finely diced

1 yellow or orange bell pepper, cored, seeded, and finely diced

1 red onion, finely chopped

⅓ cup pine nuts

1 small pack (about 1oz) of dill, finely chopped

1 small pack (about 1oz) of flat-leaf parsley, finely chopped

1 small pack (about 1oz) of mint, leaves finely chopped

finely grated zest and juice of 1 unwaxed lemon

olive oil

Maldon sea salt flakes and freshly ground black pepper

Cook the giant couscous following the package directions, then drain. Rinse thoroughly in cold water until completely cool and let drain for a few minutes.

Tip the drained couscous into a mixing bowl, then add all the remaining ingredients, drizzle in some olive oil, and season with a generous amount of salt and pepper. Stir to combine evenly, taste, and adjust the seasoning if desired, then serve.

Serve with Dried Lime & Spice-marinated Lamb Chops (see page 95).

Beet & Pomegranate Salad

One of my favorite refrigerator staples is vacuum-packed beets, which I love for their versatility and long life. Beets are so flavorsome on their own that you really don't need many other ingredients to transform them into something wonderful. Their sweet nature pairs beautifully with fresh flavors and a little acidity, so the sharp taste of pomegranate molasses works perfectly with beets, gently contrasted by refreshing sweet bursts of pomegranate seeds. This really is a beautiful salad and a perfect side for any meal.

SERVES 3 TO 4

10½oz vacuum-packed cooked beets
    in natural juice, drained

½ cup pomegranate seeds

2 scallions, thinly sliced diagonally
    from root to tip

½ small pack (about ½oz) of dill,
    coarsely chopped

2 tablespoons pomegranate molasses

1 tablespoon olive oil

1 teaspoon rice vinegar

Maldon sea salt flakes and freshly
    ground black pepper

Cut the beets into wedges or bite-sized chunks and put into a bowl.

Add all the remaining ingredients to the bowl and season with a generous amount of salt and pepper. Mix together well and serve.

Serve with Bean & Feta Patties (see page 82) or My Ultimate Ground Beef & Eggplant (see page 100).

Chicken Shawarma Salad

We go through a lot of shawarma in my house, mainly because everyone loves kebabs. But when I'm feeling like I need a lighter meal, I make my chicken shawarma salad. It has all the components of a classic shawarma but with lettuce instead of flatbread and, truth be told, I love it. I also now bake the chicken in the oven so that it's even easier to make and means I can continue doing other things around the house until it's ready. It is a wonderfully fresh, crunchy, and satisfying salad, and should you have a bigger appetite, then yes, of course, you can serve it with some wraps or flatbread on the side.

SERVES 4

For the chicken

1¼lb boneless, skinless chicken thighs

¼ cup Greek yogurt, plus extra to serve

2 teaspoons garlic granules

2 teaspoons ground cumin

2 teaspoons ground coriander

2 teaspoons paprika

2 garlic cloves, crushed

juice of ½ lemon

1 tablespoon olive oil

Maldon sea salt flakes and freshly
   ground black pepper

For the salad

1 head of lettuce, sliced

4 large tomatoes, halved and sliced

1 large red onion, halved and thinly sliced

4 to 6 large pickled cucumbers (the long
   Middle Eastern variety are ideal),
   sliced diagonally

½ small pack (about ½oz) of fresh
   cilantro, coarsely chopped, plus extra
   to garnish (optional)

juice of ½ lemon

olive oil

chilli sauce, such as Sriracha, to serve

Preheat the oven to 415°F. Line a roasting pan with parchment paper.

Put all the chicken ingredients into a mixing bowl and season generously with salt and pepper, then use your hands to mix well and ensure the marinade coats the top and underside of each thigh.

Transfer the chicken thighs to the lined pan and roast for 40 to 45 minutes until lovely and charred and cooked through. Remove from the oven, slice the cooked chicken thinly, and set aside.

Place all the salad ingredients together on a large platter. Squeeze over the lemon juice, drizzle with a little olive oil, and season well with salt and pepper. Then gently toss together, add the chicken slices, and toss again. Drizzle with the yogurt and some chilli sauce, and scatter with a little extra cilantro if desired. This needs no accompaniment.

Cauliflower & Lentil Salad

I love lentils, especially in salads. Paired here with cauliflower and some sweet and spicy ingredients, this is one of those salads you won't be able to put down. Perfect on its own or with fish, chicken, or pan-fried halloumi.

SERVES 6 TO 8

1⅓ cups uncooked green lentils

1 large cauliflower, broken into florets

olive oil

1 teaspoon paprika

1 teaspoon ground coriander

1 teaspoon ground cumin

1 teaspoon garlic granules

1 cup flaked almonds

1⅓ cups finely chopped pitted dates

2 long red chiles, seeded and finely chopped

1 small pack (about 1oz) of flat-leaf parsley, finely chopped

1 small pack (about 1oz) of fresh cilantro, finely chopped

Maldon sea salt flakes and freshly ground black pepper

For the dressing

¼ cup date molasses

3 tablespoons vegan red wine vinegar

2 tablespoons olive oil

Cook the lentils following the package directions, then drain, rinse thoroughly in cold water, drain again, and set aside.

Preheat the oven to 350°F. Line a large baking pan with parchment paper.

Place the cauliflower florets on the lined pan and drizzle generously with olive oil. Mix the spices and garlic granules together with a generous amount of salt and pepper and sprinkle over the florets, then use your hands to evenly coat them in the oil and spice mixture. Arrange them in a single layer and roast for 30 minutes, adding the flaked almonds for the last 10 minutes of the cooking time. Remove from the oven.

Mix the dressing ingredients together with a generous seasoning of salt and pepper in a small pitcher or bowl.

Put the lentils into a mixing bowl, add a little olive oil and salt and pepper, and mix together. Then add the dates, toasted flaked almonds, chiles, herbs, and dressing and mix everything together well. Decant onto a large serving platter, top with the roasted cauliflower florets, and serve.

Serve with Burnt Zucchini with Lemon & Feta Yogurt (see page 145).

Arugula Salad with Halloumi, Blood Oranges & Pistachio Nuts

Halloumi makes any dish extra special, but this particular combination really works well with salty, sweet, crunchy, and peppery components that deliver big on flavor and take no time to throw together. If you can't find blood oranges, ordinary oranges will absolutely do.

SERVES 2 TO 4

2 blood oranges

9oz block of halloumi cheese

olive oil

2½ cups loosely packed arugula leaves

½ red onion, halved and thinly sliced into half moons

¼ pistachio slivers (or very coarsely chopped whole nuts)

For the dressing

juice reserved from preparing the blood oranges

2 tablespoons vegan red wine vinegar

1 tablespoon olive oil

2 teaspoons marmalade

Maldon sea salt flakes and freshly ground black pepper

Using a sharp knife, cut a disk of peel off the top and base of each orange, then working from the top of the fruit downward, cut away the remaining peel and pith in strips, just enough to expose the orange flesh, until the entire orange is peeled. Cut each orange in half widthwise, then slice each half into half moons. Reserve any juice that is released from the oranges for the dressing.

Cut the halloumi into 7 slices and then cut each slice lengthwise into 2 fingers. Place a skillet over medium-high heat, drizzle in some olive oil, and once hot, fry the halloumi fingers for a couple of minutes on each side until they are soft but deeply golden brown. Remove from the heat.

Arrange the arugula leaves on a large plate and add the fried halloumi and orange slices, then scatter with the red onion and pistachios. Mix the dressing ingredients together in a small pitcher or bowl. Season well with salt and pepper and mix again, then pour over the salad. Serve immediately.

Serve with Bean, Bell Pepper & Thyme Khorak (see page 141).

My Platter of Dreams

This collection of wonderful things that Persians, Arabs, and Turks like to graze on really is everything I could hope to have served to me for a casual lunch with friends. All the elements are merely suggestions, but they certainly go well together and you can increase or decrease the offering and add your own twists very easily, exactly as you please. Get creative—and enjoy!

SERVES 4 TO 6

3 eggs

5½oz baby plum tomatoes, halved

½ large cucumber, diced

½ red onion, diced

olive oil

1 teaspoon dried wild oregano, plus
    extra for sprinkling

1 teaspoon pul biber chile flakes, plus
    extra for sprinkling

14oz can chickpeas, drained

2 teaspoons za'atar, plus extra to serve

juice of ½ lemon

½ packet (about ½oz) of fresh
    cilantro, finely chopped

1 cup thick Greek yogurt

7oz feta cheese, broken
    into 10 to 12 large chunks

handful of pitted Kalamata olives

handful of pitted green olives

Maldon sea salt flakes and freshly
    ground black pepper

bread, to serve (optional)

Cook the eggs in a small saucepan of boiling water for 7 minutes or so, then drain and cool under cold running water. Once they are cool enough to handle, remove the shells, halve the eggs, and set aside.

Put the tomatoes, cucumber, and onion into a mixing bowl, add some salt and pepper, a light drizzle of olive oil, the oregano and pul biber, and mix together.

In another bowl, mix the chickpeas with the za'atar, lemon juice, a light drizzle of olive oil, salt and pepper, and the cilantro.

Choose the largest platter you can find. Spoon the yogurt into a small bowl or into a corner of the platter. Arrange the tomato mixture, chickpeas, egg halves, feta, and olives on the platter, drizzle the yogurt and feta with a little extra olive oil, and sprinkle some extra oregano and pul biber wherever you like. In another small bowl, add extra za'atar mixed with a little olive oil for drizzling, and serve with bread if desired.

Serve with Mama Ghanoush (see page 158).

"Hummus" Salad

I have written many a hummus recipe in my time, but I confess, I don't like to deviate too far from the original recipe because it's so wonderful in its simplicity. Having said that, one day when my food processor died on me and the prospect of hand-mashing chickpeas did not appeal, this recipe happened. And that, dear friends, is what you call "a happy accident." All the joys and key ingredients of hummus with a few little twists, served as a salad so good in its own right that I wouldn't hesitate to serve hummus alongside it.

SERVES 2 TO 4

14oz can chickpeas, drained

2 preserved lemons, seeded and finely chopped

½ small pack (about ½oz) of flat-leaf parsley, leaves picked

olive oil, for frying

4 garlic cloves, thinly sliced

For the dressing

3 tablespoons tahini

1 teaspoon garlic granules

juice of ½ lemon

3 tablespoons warm water

Maldon sea salt flakes and freshly ground black pepper

Mix the chickpeas, preserved lemons, and parsley leaves together in a small bowl, then decant onto a serving platter.

Heat a small saucepan or skillet over medium heat and pour in about ½ inch olive oil. Line a plate with a double layer of paper towels. Once the oil is hot, add the garlic slices and swirl them around until they are nicely golden brown all over, ensuring they do not burn (if they are browning too quickly, lift the pan off the heat and swirl the pan around). Remove with a slotted spoon and transfer to the paper-lined plate to drain.

Mix the dressing ingredients, except the warm water, together in a small bowl and season very generously with salt and pepper. Once combined, slowly mix in the water until the dressing reaches a pouring consistency.

Pour the dressing over the chickpeas. Top with the crispy garlic slices, season with black pepper, and serve.

Serve with Fatayer Puffs (see page 57).

Nectarine, Halloumi & Cucumber Salad with Cashews

I just love this salad. Sweet, citrusy, salty, and crunchy, and with so much flavor packed into it that every mouthful is a different combination of happiness. It's easy to pull together and so colorful and pretty when on the plate. Best of all? It really doesn't involve much work. Perfect alongside any feast or as a lovely refreshing meal on its own.

SERVES 4

9oz block of halloumi cheese

2 ripe nectarines

½ large cucumber

generous handful of cashew nuts

2 scallions, thinly sliced diagonally
   from root to tip

olive oil

½ small pack (about ½oz) of mint,
   leaves picked, rolled up tightly, and
   thinly sliced into ribbons

½ small pack (about ½oz) of dill,
   coarsely chopped

½ teaspoon nigella seeds

½ teaspoon pul biber chile flakes

juice of ½ orange

freshly ground black pepper

Cut the block of halloumi in half lengthwise and cut each half into cubes.

Cut each nectarine in half, remove the stone, and cut the flesh into 8 pieces.

Peel the cucumber, cut in half lengthwise, and scoop the seeds out with a teaspoon. Then cut the flesh into half-moon slices about ¼ inch in thickness.

Arrange the nectarines, cucumber, cashews, and scallions on a large platter.

Heat a skillet over medium-high heat, drizzle in a little olive oil, and fry the halloumi for a couple of minutes on each side until nicely browned.

Arrange the fried halloumi in between the other ingredients on the platter and scatter with the herbs, nigella seeds, and pul biber. Season with pepper, drizzle with olive oil, and squeeze over the orange juice, then serve.

Serve with Cabbage "Bowl" Dolma (see page 147).

Pistachio Pasta Salad with Tomatoes, Olives & Red Onion

I have been making this salad for many years now using both the pistachio pesto with the recipe or—when I'm short of time and ingredients—storebought fresh basil pesto. We all make compromises sometimes, but I must admit I prefer the punchy combination of herbs in this pistachio pesto mix, brightened up even more with semi-roasted (aka sunblush or sun-dried) tomatoes and my favorite Kalamata olives and red onion. It's a lunchbox classic for me, and something I make in big quantities for the household to snack on over a few days. I also love serving it with roast chicken and as a picnic dish, too.

SERVES 4 TO 6

9oz of your favorite pasta shape

2½oz Parmesan cheese, coarsely chopped

½ cup pistachio slivers (or very coarsely chopped whole nuts)

2 garlic cloves, peeled

1 small pack (about 1oz) of dill

1 small pack (about 1oz) of fresh cilantro

1 small pack (about 1oz) of flat-leaf parsley

juice of ½ fat lemon

10½oz semi-dried tomatoes in oil, drained and oil reserved, then cut widthwise into strips

olive oil (optional)

1 red onion, halved and thinly sliced into half moons

2 to 3 generous handfuls of pitted Kalamata olives

Maldon sea salt flakes and freshly ground black pepper

Cook the pasta in a large saucepan of salted boiling water following the package directions, then drain, rinse very well in cold water until completely cooled, and let stand to continue draining.

Put the Parmesan, pistachios, garlic, and some salt and pepper into a small food processor and blitz together. Then add the herbs, lemon juice, and the oil from the tomatoes and blitz until well combined. Add more olive oil as needed to enable the pesto to spin without making it too oily.

Add the drained pasta to a mixing bowl along with the tomatoes, onion, and finally the pesto. Mix everything together, then stir in the olives. Taste and adjust the seasoning if desired. This needs no accompaniment.

Sweet & Fragrant Mushroom Salad

What may sound like a bizarre offering is actually so delicious that when I first created the recipe, I made it three days in a row. The flavors are inspired by Thailand, and the wonderful addition of toasted dry rice is an ingenious way of injecting a nutty, smoky flavor into the dish. This is great paired with some steamed rice.

SERVES 4 TO 6

2 tablespoons uncooked basmati rice

1¼lb cremino mushrooms, quartered

4 scallions, thinly sliced diagonally
   from root to tip

olive oil, for drizzling

½ red onion, halved and very thinly
   sliced into half moons

1 long red chile, seeded and very
   finely chopped

½ small pack (about ½oz) of fresh
   cilantro, coarsely chopped

½ small pack (about ½oz) of mint,
   leaves coarsely chopped

For the dressing

finely grated zest and juice of 1 fat
   unwaxed lime

1 large garlic clove, minced

2 tablespoons superfine sugar

1 tablespoon soy sauce

1 teaspoon sesame oil

freshly ground black pepper

Heat a dry skillet over medium-high heat, add the rice, and toast, shaking the pan to toss the rice, for 2 minutes, or until the rice is deep golden brown all over, but not burnt. Remove from the heat and let cool.

Heat a large skillet over high heat and, once hot, add the mushrooms to the dry pan. Let them release their liquid and then cook until the liquid has evaporated, stirring occasionally. Add a drizzle of olive oil to the pan and cook the mushrooms until browned. Remove from the heat and set aside.

Using a mortar and pestle, grind the toasted rice as finely as you can until you reach the consistency of coarse sand grains. Don't be tempted to use a spice or coffee grinder, which will produce far too fine a powder.

Mix the dressing ingredients together in a small bowl until evenly combined.

Transfer the mushrooms to a mixing bowl and add the ground rice followed by the dressing and mix together really well. Add the scallions, red onion, chile, and fresh herbs and mix again, then serve.

Serve with Roasted Vegetable & Mixed Bean Salad with Herb Dressing (see page 33).

Spice-roasted Butternut & Black Rice Salad

Big salads are among some of my favorite recipes to make. I'm not talking about limp, overdressed lettuce leaves. I mean substantial, flavorful combinations. Butternut squash has a natural sweetness and means you can throw so many bold flavors and spices at it and it just balances them out beautifully.

SERVES 6 TO 8

2¼lb butternut squash, peeled, halved, seeded, and cut into ½-inch slices

olive oil

1 teaspoon ground cumin

1 teaspoon ground cinnamon

1 teaspoon paprika

1½ cups black rice

1 large red onion, finely chopped

¾ cup dried cranberries

½ cup flaked almonds

1½ cups pomegranate seeds

1 small pack (about 1oz) of flat-leaf parsley, leaves finely chopped

Maldon sea salt flakes and freshly ground black pepper

For the dressing

3 tablespoons pomegranate molasses

3 tablespoons olive oil

2 tablespoons honey or maple syrup

1 tablespoon vegan red wine vinegar

1 teaspoon ground cinnamon

Preheat the oven to 425°F. Line a large baking pan with parchment paper.

Place the pieces of squash on the lined pan and drizzle generously with olive oil. Mix the spices together and sprinkle over the pieces, then use your hands to evenly coat them in the oil and spice mix. Arrange the pieces in a single layer, season with salt and pepper, and roast for 40 minutes or until starting to brown on the edges. Remove from the oven and let cool.

Cook the rice following the package directions, then rinse in cold water until cooled. Then drain and set aside.

Mix the onion, cranberries, flaked almonds, pomegranate seeds, and parsley (reserving a little for garnish) in a bowl, then add the rice. Mix the dressing ingredients together, pour over the salad, and stir in. Season generously with salt and pepper, mix again, and let rest for 15 minutes. Stir again, taste, and adjust the seasoning if desired. Serve with the roasted butternut arranged on top, scattered with the reserved parsley.

Serve with Ras el Hanout Sticky Spatchcock Squab (see page 118).

Roasted Vegetable & Mixed Bean Salad with Herb Dressing

This is a great way to pack vegetables into a salad, but in the laziest one-pan oven-bake kind of way! It is a lovely colorful dish to serve on its own or as part of a bigger feast. You can easily bulk the dish up by adding a grain of your choice, like brown or wild rice or barley, if you're feeding a crowd.

SERVES 3 TO 4

1 large zucchini, cut into
  ½-inch thick slices

1 large eggplant, peeled and cut into
  about ¾-inch chunks

1 large red bell pepper, seeded and cut
  lengthwise into ½-inch thick strips

olive oil

1 small red onion, finely chopped

14oz can black beans, drained and
  rinsed

14oz can cannellini beans, drained
  and rinsed

For the herb dressing

good squeeze of lemon juice

½ small pack (about ½oz) of parsley

½ small pack (about ½oz) of fresh
  cilantro

2 garlic cloves

¼ teaspoon dried red chile flakes

1 tablespoon vegan red wine vinegar

1 heaped teaspoon superfine sugar

Maldon sea salt flakes and freshly
  ground black pepper

Preheat the oven to 425°F. Line your largest baking pan with parchment paper.

Place the zucchini, eggplant, and red bell pepper on the pan, drizzle with olive oil, and use your hands to coat the vegetables in oil, adding a little more if needed. Arrange in a single layer and roast for 30 to 35 minutes or until the vegetables are cooked through. Remove from the oven and let cool.

Add all the dressing ingredients, plus 5 to 6 tablespoons olive oil, to a bullet blender or food processor. Blitz until smooth, ensuring the garlic has blended. Taste and adjust the seasoning if desired.

Tip the cooked vegetables into a mixing bowl and add the chopped onion along with the drained black and cannellini beans. Add the dressing, mix well, then taste and adjust the seasoning, if desired, before serving.

Serve with Butterflied Lamb with Tahini Garlic Yogurt (see page 123).

Tuna, Tomato & Borlotti Bean Salad

I could quite simply enjoy the combination of tuna and beans with nothing more than some onion, salt, pepper, and olive oil. But this salad is a riot of flavor that you will return to again and again. Leftovers make great packed lunches the next day, when the flavors will have intensified even more.

SERVES 6 TO 8

3 x 5oz cans tuna in oil, drained

2 x 14oz cans borlotti beans, drained and rinsed

1 large red onion, finely chopped

1 small pack (about 1oz) of flat-leaf parsley, finely chopped

9oz semi-dried tomatoes in oil, drained and oil reserved, then coarsely chopped

9oz baby plum tomatoes, sliced into thirds

juice of ½ lemon

1 heaped teaspoon garlic granules

1 heaped teaspoon pul biber chile flakes

Maldon sea salt flakes and freshly ground black pepper

Put all the ingredients, except the oil from the tomatoes, into a mixing bowl and season generously with salt and pepper.

Add 2 to 3 tablespoons of the tomato oil to the bowl, mix well, and serve. This needs no accompaniment.

Spicy Beef, Cucumber & Herb Salad

I do love my seared beef salads, and I have made quite a few variations over the years simply because they are something I eat a lot of at home. Beef is very much the favorite, but you could use lamb or pork steaks, so go with whichever you prefer. The flavor combinations here are bold, refreshing, and really pleasing.

SERVES 2

olive oil

10½oz sirloin or porterhouse steak, cut into ½-inch cubes

generous handful of fresh cilantro

generous handful of basil leaves

generous handful of dill

½ red onion, halved and thinly sliced into half moons

½ large cucumber, peeled, halved lengthwise, and seeded, then cut into slices ¼ inch in thickness

¼ cup pomegranate seeds

Maldon sea salt flakes and freshly ground black pepper

For the dressing

1 long red chile, seeded (or not, if you prefer) and very finely chopped

1 fat garlic clove

finely grated zest and juice of 1 fat unwaxed lime

2 tablespoons olive oil

1 heaped teaspoon coriander seeds

1 tablespoon honey

Heat a skillet over high heat. Drizzle a little olive oil onto the steak pieces and rub it in to coat them all over, then season well with pepper. Once the pan is hot, add the steak pieces to the pan and season with salt. Without stirring, let the steak pieces cook lightly for just under a minute on each side. Shake the pan vigorously, then remove from the heat.

Put all the dressing ingredients (except for the honey) and some salt and pepper into a bullet blender or mini food processor and blitz until smooth. Then add the honey and mix until evenly combined.

Coarsely chop all the herbs and add them to a mixing bowl along with the steak pieces, red onion, cucumber, pomegranate seeds, and dressing and toss together well, then serve. This needs no accompaniment.

Curried Potato Salad

I'm fairly sure I have made more than a dozen different versions of potato salad over the years to appease my mother and her love for it, but this is altogether quite different and a nice change from the classic version. Curried anything is generally enough to lure me to eat something, but potatoes and curry spice are a great match. The crème fraîche is a great swap for mayonnaise. It's creamier, but somehow feels lighter and has a gentle acidity that works well with the potatoes, too.

SERVES 6 TO 8

1lb 10oz baby new potatoes

1 bunch of scallions, thinly sliced
    from root to tip

1 cup crème fraîche (or sour cream)

2 garlic cloves, crushed

2 green chiles, seeded, very finely chopped

1 tablespoon superfine sugar

1 heaped tablespoon medium curry powder

1 small pack (about 1oz) of fresh cilantro,
    finely chopped (reserve a handful for
    garnish)

2 tablespoons olive oil

Maldon sea salt flakes and freshly ground
    black pepper

Cook the potatoes whole in a saucepan of boiling water for about 15 minutes until cooked through and tender. Drain and rinse in cold water until cool. Coarsely chop the potatoes.

Put the potatoes into a mixing bowl, then add all the remaining ingredients and a generous amount of salt and pepper. Mix everything together really well and serve scattered with chopped cilantro.

Serve with My Tender TFC (see page 99) or Pan-fried Salmon with Barberry Butter (see page 133).

'Warm Harissa, Broccolini & Black Rice Salad,

I love using black rice in recipes because, whatever you add to it, it provides a beautiful contrast to the colors of the other ingredients, not to mention its pleasingly nutty and chewy texture. This is a quick throw-together using ingredients I keep handy at home. The result is fantastic. It's sweet, crunchy, spicy, and just a little zingy, too, and definitely one to remember when you want a simple yet delicious accompaniment to your meal.

SERVES 3 TO 4

1 cup black rice

7oz broccolini

7oz semi-dried tomatoes in oil, drained (reserve the oil), then cut into strips

1 tablespoon rose harissa

finely grated zest and juice of 1 unwaxed lemon

1 heaped tablespoon honey (if vegan, use maple syrup)

Maldon sea salt flakes and freshly ground black pepper

Cook the rice following the package directions.

Meanwhile, bring a saucepan of water to a boil, add the broccolini, and cook for 6 minutes. Drain, cut into bite-sized pieces, and put into a mixing bowl.

Add the tomatoes and 2 to 3 tablespoons of the reserved oil to the bowl and mix well. Then add the harissa and lemon zest and juice, and season generously with salt and pepper.

Once the rice is cooked, drain if necessary and add it to the broccolini and tomato mixture. Add the honey (or maple syrup), mix together well, and serve.

Serve with Smoked Eggplants with Lime & Maple Dressing (see page 142).

Warm Orzo, Black-eyed Pea & Herb Salad

I love pasta and I love legumes, and this recipe combines them beautifully with the addition of an abundance of fragrant herbs, which elevates the dish to another level. I'm not really sure if it's a salad or a warm bean dish, but it is definitely something I don't want to stop dipping my spoon into before serving. It really is that delicious.

SERVES 4 TO 6

1 cup orzo pasta

olive oil

2 garlic cloves, crushed

3 tablespoons tomato paste

14oz can black-eyed peas, drained and rinsed

1 small pack (about 1oz) of flat-leaf parsley, finely chopped

1 small pack (about 1oz) of dill, finely chopped

1 small pack (about 1oz) of fresh cilantro, finely chopped

1 small pack (about 1oz) of chives, thinly sliced

juice of ½ lemon

Maldon sea salt flakes and freshly ground black pepper

Cook the orzo in a large saucepan of salted boiling water following the package directions, then drain and return to the pan, but turn the heat off.

Drizzle generously with olive oil and add the garlic and tomato paste, then work into the orzo until evenly combined. Season well with salt and pepper and add the beans, chopped herbs, and lemon juice and mix well. Taste and adjust the seasoning, if desired, then serve.

Serve with Charred Broccoli with Lemons, Chiles & Yogurt (see page 154).

Watermelon, Belgian Endive & Ricotta Salad

By now you must know that I adore fresh fruit in salads, and watermelon feels especially right to me because Persians (and indeed Turks, Greeks, and Arabs) love it so much. This is perhaps a little unorthodox as a combination, but the sweet watermelon, slightly bitter Belgian Endive, and creamy ricotta work so well with the dressing to ensure that every bite is juicy and refreshing, with a lovely creaminess on the finish from the ricotta. It's simple, colorful, and flavorful—my three favorite characteristics combined.

SERVES 4 TO 6

2 heads of red and green Belgian
    endive, leaves separated
¾lb watermelon flesh, cut into
    1-inch cubes
1 cup ricotta cheese
¾ cup walnuts
1 teaspoon pul biber chile flakes
handful of mint, leaves picked,
    rolled up tightly, and thinly sliced
    into ribbons

For the dressing
finely grated zest and juice of 1 fat
    unwaxed lime
2 tablespoons honey
1 tablespoon olive oil
Maldon sea salt flakes and freshly
    ground black pepper

Arrange theBelgian endive leaves and watermelon on a large platter. Dot with dollops of the ricotta all over and scatter with the walnuts.

Mix the dressing ingredients together with a generous seasoning of salt and pepper in a small pitcher or bowl, then pour over the salad.

Sprinkle with the pul biber and finish with the mint to serve.

Serve with Ras el Hanout Sticky Spatchcock Squab (see page 118).

Vermicelli with Shrimp, Orange & Pomegranate, Tamarind & Herbs

This refreshing noodle salad has bags of flavor in every bite. You might think it strange to combine oranges and pomegranates with shrimp, but you'd be wrong. Those little bursts of sweetness work perfectly with the sharpness of the dressing, and the fresh herbs make the whole dish look like a work of art.

SERVES 2 TO 4

3½oz rice vermicelli

1 orange

5½oz cooked peeled jumbo shrimp

½ red onion, halved and thinly sliced into half moons

4 scallions, thinly sliced from root to tip

½ cup pomegranate seeds

½ small pack (about ½oz) of fresh cilantro, finely chopped

½ small pack (about ½oz) of mint, leaves picked, rolled up tightly and thinly sliced into ribbons

For the dressing

2 tablespoons olive oil

1 tablespoon tamarind paste

2 tablespoons superfine sugar

1 fat garlic clove, minced

1 teaspoon pul biber chile flakes

Maldon sea salt flakes and freshly ground black pepper

Cook the vermicelli following the package directions, then drain, plunge into cold water until completely cooled and drain again. Set aside.

Using a sharp knife, cut a disk of peel off the top and base of the orange, then working from the top of the fruit downward, cut away the remaining peel and pith in strips, just enough to expose the orange flesh, until the entire orange is peeled. Cut the orange in half widthwise, then cut each half into half moons.

Mix the dressing ingredients together in a large mixing bowl until well combined.

Add the vermicelli, oranges, and the remaining ingredients to the bowl containing the dressing and mix everything together. Taste and adjust the seasoning, if desired, then serve. This needs no accompaniment.

Light Bites
& Savory
Treats

Carrot, Oregano & Feta Börek Swirls

Börek are versatile enough to accommodate a variety of different fillings. Classic fillings are usually ground lamb, cheese, or spinach. However, this carrot, oregano, and feta börek is not only delicious but also really quite beautiful and, I'm pleased to say, really easy to make.

MAKES 6

2¼lb carrots, peeled and chopped into ½-inch pieces

olive oil

1 teaspoon dried wild oregano

7oz feta cheese, crumbled

1 small pack (about 1oz) of fresh oregano, leaves coarsely chopped

6 sheets of filo pastry

½ stick butter, melted

Maldon sea salt flakes and freshly ground black pepper

arugula salad, to serve

Preheat the oven to 425°F. Line a large baking pan with parchment paper.

Place the carrots on the lined pan. Drizzle with olive oil, season with salt and pepper, scatter with the dried oregano, and then coat the carrot pieces evenly in the oil and seasonings. Spread the carrots out on the pan and roast for 30 to 35 minutes or until starting to brown and char around the edges. Remove from the oven and let cool.

Put the feta, fresh oregano, a generous amount of black pepper, and the cooled carrots into a large mixing bowl and mix together.

Line your large baking pan with fresh parchment paper. Lay a filo sheet lengthwise on a clean work surface or cutting board. Divide the carrot mixture into 6 equal portions. Form a portion into a long sausage shape near the bottom long edge of the filo, leaving a generous 1-inch border clear at either end. Carefully, but very loosely, roll the pastry up to make a long cigar and seal the edge with melted butter. Coil the cigar into a snail shape without tightening the looseness of the pastry but squeezing and cupping it gently to keep it loose as you curve it around. Place on the lined pan and brush butter all over the exposed edges, aiming to seal any broken bits using the butter and bits of pastry from the ends. Repeat with the remaining filo sheets and carrot mixture.

Bake for 22 to 25 minutes until nicely golden brown. Remove from the oven and serve with an arugula salad.

Serve with Tangy Pomegranate & Tomato Eggplant (see page 185).

Zucchini, Lemon, Feta & Pine Nut Tart

This is one of those quick and easy recipes that can be thrown together in next to no time. No special skills or equipment are needed, just a little patience while the tart bakes and cools down enough for you to enjoy it. I love this kind of dish with a leafy green salad and a simple vinaigrette on the side, but you can also cut it into smaller portions and serve it as snacks or light bites with drinks, too.

SERVES 4

7oz feta cheese, finely crumbled

1 cup ricotta cheese

1 teaspoon dried mint

1 teaspoon dried wild oregano

2 teaspoons lemon extract

finely grated zest of 1 unwaxed lemon

1 x 11oz ready-rolled puff pastry sheet
   (about 14 x 9 inches)

1 zucchini, very thinly sliced

olive oil

handful of pine nuts

2 tablespoons honey

½ teaspoon pul biber chile flakes
   (omit if you prefer)

Maldon sea salt flakes and freshly
   ground black pepper

Preheat the oven to 425°F. Line a large baking pan with parchment paper.

Put the feta, ricotta, dried herbs, and lemon extract and zest into a mixing bowl with a good seasoning of salt and pepper. Beat together until smooth.

Place the puff pastry sheet on the lined pan and score a border ½ an inch wide around the edges, then spread the cheese mixture across the pastry up to the scored border.

Lay the zucchini slices, slightly overlapping, on the cheese mixture, season well with salt and pepper, and drizzle with olive oil. Scatter with the pine nuts and bake for 16 to 18 minutes until the pastry edges are nicely browned.

Remove from the oven and let cool slightly, then drizzle with the honey and sprinkle with the pul biber before serving.

Serve with Roasted Tomatoes with Labneh & Sumac Spice Oil (see page 177).

Curried Cheese & Potato Puffs

Bringing three of my favorite elements together—cheese, potatoes, and pastry—seems a total no-brainer for a girl like me. But the really wonderful addition is the curry powder. It just works so well with the potato and cheese, and makes these little puffs absolutely irresistible. These are the ultimate snack.

MAKES 8

9oz Russet potatoes, peeled and
    halved if large
2 tablespoons medium curry powder
¾ cup firmly packed grated sharp
    Cheddar cheese
1 x 11oz ready-rolled puff pastry sheet
    (about 14 x 9 inches)

1 beaten egg or milk, for glazing
½ teaspoon nigella seeds
Maldon sea salt flakes and freshly
    ground black pepper
Sriracha or chilli sauce, to serve

Cook the potatoes in a saucepan of boiling water for 25 to 30 minutes or until cooked through. Drain and let cool completely.

Put the cooled potatoes into a mixing bowl, add the curry powder and a very generous amount of salt and pepper. Mash it all into the potatoes, then stir in the cheese to combine.

Divide the potato mixture into 8 portions and form each into a ball, then let chill in the refrigerator for at least an hour.

Preheat the oven to 425°F. Line a large baking pan with parchment paper.

Cut the pastry sheet in half lengthwise, then cut each half into 4 squares to make 8 in total. Place a ball of cheese and potato mixture on a pastry square, then work quickly to bring all 4 corners together in the center, pinch the edges together, and twist the tops to seal. Place on the lined pan. Repeat with the remaining cheese and potato mixture and pastry.

Brush all over with a little beaten egg or milk to glaze and sprinkle nigella seeds on top. Bake for 18 minutes until nicely browned, then serve with Sriracha or chilli sauce. These need no accompaniment.

Fatayer Puffs

When I want to feed people, I like to make a wide array of dishes including *fatayer*, but I don't always have time to make fresh pastry. So, storebought pastry is the way forward. I rather like the lighter, flaky nature of puff pastry. The traditional *fatayer*, while perfectly delicious, has a chewier, somewhat weightier pastry dough. Now, I know the spice mix here looks excessive, but it is authentic, so do yourself a favour and double (or quadruple) the batch to save time when you next make these, because these little puffs are utterly delicious and you will definitely want to make them again.

MAKES 8

vegetable oil

9oz ground lamb

1 heaped teaspoon garlic granules

¼ teaspoon paprika

¼ teaspoon ground cumin

¼ teaspoon ground coriander

¼ teaspoon ground cloves

¼ teaspoon ground cinnamon

⅛ teaspoon ground nutmeg

⅛ teaspoon cayenne pepper

½ small pack (about ½oz) of flat-leaf
   parsley, finely chopped

2 tablespoons pine nuts

1 x 11oz ready-rolled puff pastry sheet
   (about 14 x 9 inches)

1 egg, beaten

Maldon sea salt flakes and freshly
   ground black pepper

Place a large skillet over high heat, add a little drizzle of vegetable oil followed by the ground lamb, and immediately break it up as finely as possible to prevent it from cooking in clumps. Continue cooking the ground lamb, stirring as you go, until just cooked through but not browned. Add the garlic granules, all the spices, and a generous amount of salt and pepper followed by the parsley and stir-fry for a further 5 minutes. Remove from the heat and let cool. Add the pine nuts and mix well.

Preheat the oven to 425°F. Line a large baking pan with parchment paper.

Cut the puff pastry sheet in half widthwise, then cut each half into quarters to make 8 rectangles in total. Divide the mixture into 8 equal portions. Form a portion into a mini sausage shape in the center of a pastry rectangle, then pinch the pastry at either end and twist to seal and create mini boat shapes. Place on the lined baking pan. Repeat with the remaining meat mixture and pastry rectangles. Brush the pastries with beaten egg to glaze and bake for 20 to 22 minutes, or until the pastry is golden brown. Remove from the oven and serve.

Serve with "Hummus" Salad (see page 22).

Halloumi Airbags

Don't let the recipe title put you off because until you make them, you won't know what I mean. These lovely little halloumi and herb pastries inflate when you fry them, making them feather-light, crisp, and delicious. They are best enjoyed freshly made, so fry them just before you intend to eat them.

MAKES 16

9oz block of halloumi cheese, coarsely grated

1 small pack (about 1oz) of flat-leaf parsley, finely chopped

1 small pack (about 1oz) of dill, finely chopped

2 teaspoons dried mint

vegetable oil, for frying

2 sheets of filo pastry (each about 19 x 10 inches)

1 egg, beaten

freshly ground black pepper

Put the halloumi, fresh herbs, and dried mint into a mixing bowl with a generous amount of black pepper, stir to combine, then set aside.

Heat a large skillet with high sides (or a Dutch oven) over medium-high heat, pour in about 1 inch of vegetable oil and bring to frying temperature. (Add a small piece of filo pastry. If it sizzles immediately, the oil is hot enough.) Line a baking pan with a double layer of paper towel.

Cut each filo pastry sheet into 8 squares. Divide the halloumi mixture into 16 equal portions. Place a portion on a filo square, positioned diamond-wise, then brush 2 adjacent edges of the diamond with beaten egg, fold over the filling to form a triangle, and press the edges together to seal. Repeat with the remaining halloumi mixture and filo squares. Pinch each airbag tightly around the edges.

Add the airbags to the hot oil and fry in batches for a minute on each side until they puff up and turn golden brown. Remove with a slotted spoon and transfer to the paper-lined plate to drain, then serve. These need no accompaniment.

Lamb & Cilantro Dumplings

There isn't a single dumpling, in sauce or soup, that I couldn't love, whether fried, steamed, or boiled. I adore them all. The filling I've created here is a punchy little number, but that is very much how I like it.

MAKES 18

vegetable oil, for frying

1¼ cups all-purpose flour, plus extra for dusting

2 to 3 pinches of Maldon sea salt flakes, crumbled

½ cup boiling water, or more if needed

1 tablespoon cumin seeds

½ teaspoon dried red chile flakes

9oz ground lamb

½ small pack (about ½oz) of fresh cilantro, very finely chopped

1 tablespoon rice vinegar

2 garlic cloves, crushed

¼ cup cold water

Maldon sea salt flakes and freshly ground black pepper

Sriracha or light soy sauce for dipping, to serve

To make the dough, mix the flour and salt together in a bowl, add the boiling water, and mix with a fork until it comes together into a dough (adding a little more boiling water if needed). Dust a work surface with flour. Knead the dough for 2 minutes, return to the bowl, cover with plastic wrap, and let stand for 20 minutes.

Meanwhile, for the filling, heat a dry skillet over medium-high heat, add the cumin seeds, and toast for 1 to 2 minutes until they release their aroma, shaking the pan intermittently to prevent them from burning. Remove from the heat and stir in the chile flakes while still hot, then grind together in a mortar and pestle.

Put the remaining ingredients, except the vegetable oil, into a mixing bowl. Add the ground cumin and chile and season very well with salt and pepper. Then use your hands to combine the ingredients really well until you have an evenly smooth paste. Weigh the mixture and divide it into 18 equal portions.

Once the dough has rested, dust a baking pan with a little extra flour. Form the dough into one long sausage shape and divide into 18 balls. Roll out each ball into a disk about 3¼ inches in diameter, place on the pan, and cover with a clean damp dish cloth. Set aside until you need them.

To make the dumplings, place a portion of the lamb filling on a dough disk and fold one side of the dough over it to form a semicircle. Seal and crimp the edges by pressing with the tines of a fork. Stand them with the seam upright so they form a flat base. Repeat with the remaining dough disks and filling.

Heat a large skillet over medium-high heat, drizzle in some vegetable oil, and fry half the dumplings for about 2 to 3 minutes until the bottoms start to turn golden. Pour in the cold water and shake the pan gently. Cover and cook for 6 to 8 minutes until well browned and crispy on the bottom. Remove from the pan and repeat the process with the remaining dumplings. Serve with the dipping sauce of your choice.

Herb & Spice Feta,

These feta balls are simple enough to make, but I chose four different flavorings to give them a little extra dimension. Enjoy them in salads or even on their own with lovely a warm pillowy bread that's good for mopping, or flatbreads or wraps. They also make a wonderful gift, so prepare a double batch if you think you can stand to part with a jar. The feta keeps for up to a week submerged in oil in a sealed jar in the fridge.

SERVES 2 TO 4

7oz block of feta cheese, cut into 12

1 teaspoon sumac

1½ teaspoons dried wild oregano

2 teaspoons pul biber chile flakes

2 teaspoons nigella seeds

extra virgin olive oil

flatbread or wraps, to serve

Shape the feta pieces into balls using your hands, then roll three of the balls in one of the four spices until evenly coated all over. Repeat with the remaining balls and spices. Arrange them on a small serving plate, drizzle with extra virgin olive oil, and serve with flatbread or wraps.

Alternatively, place the coated feta in a clean airtight jar and pour in enough of the oil to cover them. Seal the lid tightly, then refrigerate until required.

Serve with Beet & Pomegranate Salad (see page 13) or My Platter of Dreams (see page 21).

Chicken Wings with Tamarind

What can I say? I'm a sucker for chicken wings. I don't really know why wings do it for me the way no other part of a chicken ever could, but the real bonus is that they are cheap and cheerful and—when cooked properly—can beat beef tenderloin, in my humble opinion, any day. My favorite flavor profiles for wings are either spicy or sweet and sticky, though even better is the two aforementioned combined. Tamarind is one of those unapologetically sour ingredients from the East that is often misunderstood in the West, but when you balance its sharpness with a little sweetness, it's wonderfully satisfying.

SERVES 4

2¼lb chicken wings

2 level tablespoons baking powder

Maldon sea salt flakes and freshly
    ground black pepper

2 scallions, thinly sliced diagonally
    from root to tip, to garnish

For the sauce

3 tablespoons tamarind paste

2 tablespoons warm water

⅓ cup honey

1 teaspoon pul biber chile flakes,
    plus extra to garnish (optional)

Preheat the oven to 400°F. Line your largest roasting pan with parchment paper.

Put the chicken wings into a mixing bowl, add the baking powder and a very generous amount of salt and pepper and massage really well into the wings as best you can. Spread the wings out on the lined roasting pan and bake for 30 minutes. Then increase the oven temperature to 500°F (or your highest setting), and bake for a further 25 minutes until nicely browned and cooked through.

Meanwhile, place the sauce ingredients along with a gentle seasoning of salt in a small saucepan over very low heat and stir until evenly combined and gently bubbling. Remove from the heat and set aside.

Transfer the baked wings to a clean mixing bowl and pour the sauce over them, ensuring you coat each wing. Serve garnished with the scallions and a little extra pul biber if desired.

Serve with Spice-roasted Potatoes with Bell Pepper, Tomato & Harissa Sauce (see page 166) or Nut Butter Noodles (see page 204).

Ground Lamb & Cheddar Tortillas

This is the kind of quick and easy food that everyone in my household loves. I've been blessed with stepkids who thankfully like spice, and these quesadilla-inspired filled tortillas are a big win for them and an even bigger relief for me. The recipe comes together quickly and can be eaten sliced for snacks, or with your favorite salads or vegetables to make a proper meal. Use any ground meat plus any cheese you like, but I do feel that the tang of a good sharp Cheddar works really well with the spices here.

SERVES 2 TO 4

vegetable oil

9oz ground lamb

1 teaspoon garlic granules

1 teaspoon ground cumin

1 teaspoon paprika

2 tablespoons tomato paste

½ pack (about ½oz) of flat-leaf parsley, finely chopped

2 large tortilla wraps

¾ cup grated sharp Cheddar cheese

Maldon sea salt flakes and freshly ground black pepper

For the harissa yogurt (optional)

¾ cup Greek yogurt

1 tablespoon harissa

Place a skillet over high heat, add a little drizzle of vegetable oil followed by the ground lamb along with the garlic granules and all the spices. Immediately break up the ground lamb as finely as possible to prevent it from cooking in clumps while you work in the flavorings. Add the tomato paste and a generous amount of salt and pepper. Stir-fry for 5 minutes, then add the parsley and stir-fry for another couple of minutes until the ground lamb is fully cooked. Set aside.

To make the harissa yogurt (if using), pour the yogurt into a small bowl and stir through the harissa just enough to create a marble effect. Set aside.

Heat a large skillet over medium heat, place a tortilla in the dry pan, and scatter with half the grated Cheddar. Using a slotted spoon (to avoid any excess grease), add half the ground lamb onto one half of the tortilla. Check that the underside of the tortilla is toasting nicely, and when ready, fold the half without the lamb over the filling. Remove from the pan and repeat with the remaining ingredients. Cut the filled tortillas into portions and serve with the harissa yogurt if desired. These need no accompaniment.

Mushroom Cigar Börek

I do love the therapeutic element of making *sigara börek*. Gently stuffing and rolling them can be quite soothing, as long as you aren't in a hurry. While this filling is not a traditional one, mushrooms work well with spice and have their own distinctly earthy flavor, which is perfect as a meat alternative. I would usually brush my börek with beaten egg or butter for crunch, gloss, and richness, but I wanted to keep this recipe friendly for people of every dietary description. So, I used a little oil instead and it works just as well.

MAKES 16

1lb 2oz cremino mushrooms, halved and thinly sliced

olive oil

1 teaspoon garlic granules

2 teaspoons za'atar

1 teaspoon pul biber chile flakes

4 sheets of filo pastry (each about 19 x 10 inches)

1 teaspoon nigella seeds

Maldon sea salt flakes and freshly ground black pepper

Heat a large skillet over medium-high heat, and once hot, add the mushrooms to the dry pan. Let them release their liquid and then cook for 4 to 5 minutes until all the liquid has evaporated, stirring occasionally. Add a drizzle of olive oil followed by the garlic granules, spices, and a good seasoning of salt and pepper. Stir-fry for 3 to 4 minutes, then remove from the heat and let cool.

Preheat the oven to 425°F. Line a large baking pan with parchment paper.

Cut the filo pastry sheets in half widthwise, then cut each in half to make 16 long strips in total. Divide the mushroom mixture into 16 equal portions. Pour 2 to 3 tablespoons olive oil into a little bowl. Place a portion of the mushroom mixture near the bottom of a pastry strip, then fold the bottom edge up over the filling. Begin rolling up the pastry loosely. When you reach halfway, fold the sides of the pastry strip into the middle and continue rolling up. Using a pastry brush, seal the end of the pastry with a little oil. Place the pastry cigar, seam-side down, on the lined baking pan. Repeat with the remaining mushroom mixture and filo strips.

Brush the pastry cigars all over with olive oil and scatter with the nigella seeds. Bake for 20 to 22 minutes, or until golden brown. Remove from the oven and let cool slightly before serving.

Serve with Mama Ghanoush (see page 158).

My Sweet, Salty & Sublime 'BHT

I never thought that combining two salty ingredients would work so well. Then I added juicy tomatoes and sweet harissa ketchup to bacon and halloumi, stuffed it all in fresh pitta bread pockets, and it came together beautifully. No disrespect to the BLT, but the BHT is the kind of thing I could eat for breakfast, lunch, and dinner. It hits every spot it should.

SERVES 2

4 strips of bacon

2 tomatoes, thin disk trimmed from the top and base of each, then cut into thick slices

1 teaspoon dried wild oregano

olive oil

9oz block of halloumi cheese, cut into 6 slices

2 pitta breads

freshly ground black pepper

For the sauce

2 tablespoons tomato ketchup

1 tablespoon rose harissa

Line a plate with a double layer of paper towels. Heat a skillet over high heat and fry the bacon until crisp on both sides. Remove and transfer to the paper-lined plate to drain.

Wipe the pan clean and place over medium-high heat. Season both sides of the tomato slices with the oregano and pepper, drizzle a little oil into the skillet, and fry the tomato slices for 1 to 2 minutes on each side until charred. Remove from the pan and set aside.

Drizzle a little more oil into the pan and fry the halloumi slices for a few minutes on both sides until deep golden brown.

Meanwhile, mix the sauce ingredients together in a small bowl.

Open up the pitta bread pockets, divide the bacon, halloumi, tomatoes, and then the sauce between them and serve. This needs no accompaniment.

Spicy Keema Rolls

The filling in these little rolls wouldn't be out of place in a samosa, and these are my way of satisfying any craving I might have for one. The recipe makes eight, but you could, of course, use a few more sheets of filo pastry and make them slightly smaller as part of a bigger feast. They also work really well with finely chopped mixed vegetables. For a vegan version, you can ditch the egg in favor of water to bind the mixture and glaze them with oil instead. Serve with mango chutney or your favorite sweet dipping sauce.

MAKES 8

vegetable oil

1 large onion, finely chopped

1 teaspoon cumin seeds

1lb 2oz ground beef

1 teaspoon ground turmeric

1 tablespoon pul biber chile flakes

1 tablespoon garlic granules

generous handful of frozen peas

1 small pack (about 1oz) of fresh
   cilantro, finely chopped

4 sheets of filo pastry (each about
   19 x 10 inches)

1 egg, beaten

Maldon sea salt flakes and freshly
   ground black pepper

Preheat the oven to 425°F. Line a large baking pan with parchment paper.

Heat a large skillet over medium-high heat, drizzle in some vegetable oil, and fry the onion until softened. Add the cumin seeds and continue frying until the onion is nicely browned.

Add the ground beef and break it up as finely as you can to prevent it from cooking in clumps, folding it into the onion. Add the spices and garlic granules and a generous amount of salt and pepper and stir well. Continue cooking until the beef is just cooked through but not browned, stirring as you go. Then stir in the peas and cook for a couple of minutes before adding the cilantro and cooking for a couple more minutes. Remove from the heat and let cool.

Cut each filo pastry sheet in half widthwise to make 8 squares in total. Divide the meat mixture into 8 equal portions. Place a portion near the bottom edge of a filo square, then fold in the sides and bottom edge up over the filling. Begin rolling up the pastry, tucking in the edges on each side as you go. Once you have reached halfway, brush the exposed pastry edge with beaten egg and finish rolling up, then seal the edge. Place, seam-side down, on the lined baking pan. Repeat with the rest of the meat mixture and filo squares. Brush with beaten egg to glaze and bake for 20 to 22 minutes, or until golden brown. Remove from the oven and serve.

Serve with Ras el Hanout & Sweet Potatoes with Tahini Yogurt & Herb Oil (see page 165) or Roasted Eggplants with Spicy Peanut Sauce (see page 173).

Sabich

I first heard of *sabich* (pronounced sab-eekh), an Iraqi–Jewish sandwich usually eaten for breakfast and now very popular in Israel, while filming a food show in Canada. This wonderful eggplant sandwich has all the makings of one of the greatest meatless sandwiches I have ever tasted. Traditionally, it is served with *amba* sauce, a sharp mango sauce. This is hard to find, so I raided my store cupboard and dug out the mango chutney and added the sharp tang of lime juice, which did the job perfectly.

SERVES 4

3 eggplants, peeled and cut into slices ½ inch in thickness

olive oil, for brushing

1 teaspoon ground cumin

1 teaspoon ground coriander

1 teaspoon garlic granules

½ cucumber, cut into ½-inch cubes

2 tomatoes, diced

1 small red onion, halved and thinly sliced into half moons

½ packet (about ½oz) of fresh cilantro, coarsely chopped

½ packet (about ½oz) of mint, leaves coarsely chopped

Maldon sea salt flakes and freshly ground black pepper

To serve

⅓ cup mango chutney

juice of 1 lime

¼ cup Greek yogurt

4 pitta breads

2 soft-cooked eggs, halved

Preheat the oven to 400°F. Line a large baking pan with parchment paper.

Place the eggplant slices on the lined pan and brush both sides generously with olive oil. Mix the spices and garlic granules together, then sprinkle over both sides. Season both sides with salt and pepper, and then pat the seasoning into the eggplant. Roast for 30 minutes without turning them over.

Meanwhile, mix the cucumber, tomatoes, onion, and herbs together with some salt and pepper in a bowl. Mix the mango chutney and lime juice together in a separate bowl.

To serve, season the yogurt with salt and pepper, then open up the pitta bread pockets. Spread the inside of the pockets with the yogurt and then divide the roasted eggplant between each, followed by the salad, mango sauce, and half a soft-cooked egg. Drizzle with a little extra yogurt to finish.

Serve with Beet & Pomegranate Salad (see page 13) or "Hummus" Salad (see page 22).

Cod Flavor Bombs

These delightful little cod bites are exactly what the name says they are. They just burst with flavor! I love fish fritters, cakes, dumplings, and the like, and could easily eat a dozen of these bombs in one sitting. To make more of a meal of them, you can add them to hot dog buns or wraps with some salad and your favorite sauce for the ultimate satisfaction. Try them with chilli sauce or mayo flavored with harissa and lime.

SERVES 2 TO 4

1lb 2oz boneless, skinless cod (or other white fish), cut into about 1-inch cubes

2 teaspoons ground coriander

2 teaspoons pul biber chile flakes

2 teaspoons dried wild oregano

1 unwaxed lemon

vegetable oil, for frying

Maldon sea salt flakes and freshly ground black pepper

juice of ½ lemon (use the leftover lemon above)

For the batter

½ stick butter, melted and cooled

2 eggs

1½ cups all-purpose flour

1 teaspoon pul biber chile flakes

1 teaspoon ground coriander

1 teaspoon dried wild oregano

1 cup cold beer (or sparkling water)

To serve

lime wedges

your favorite sauce

Put the cod into a mixing bowl. Add the spices, oregano, and a generous amount of salt and pepper. Finely grate over the zest of the lemon, drizzle with half the lemon juice, and mix well to coat the fish.

In another bowl, beat the melted butter and eggs together, then add the flour, spices, oregano, and a generous amount of salt and pepper and add the beer (or sparkling water). Use a wire whisk to beat everything together gently until you have a smooth batter. Do no overbeat the batter otherwise it will be heavy.

Heat a large skillet with high sides (or a Dutch oven) over medium-high heat, pour in about 1 inch of vegetable oil and bring to frying temperature. (Add a little bit of the batter. If it sizzles immediately, the oil is hot enough.) Line a plate with a double layer of paper towels.

Dip each piece of cod in turn into the batter, then carefully lower into the hot oil and fry in batches for 2 to 3 minutes or until crispy and deep golden brown. Remove with a slotted spoon and transfer to the paper-lined plate to drain. Enjoy with a good squeeze of lime juice and your favorite sauce.

Serve with Curried Potato Salad (see page 38).

Spicy Shrimp Fritters

I have always thought of shrimp as a really useful, convenient ingredient to keep in the freezer, ready for making pastas, rice dishes, soups, dumplings, and stir-fries. These shrimp fritters are utterly delicious and ideal for snacking or serving with drinks, but are also great as part of a bigger meal. They are really easy to make and don't take much effort or time to cook, which makes them the perfect go-to time and again when in a pinch. Shrimp are highly versatile and work with a myriad of different spices and ingredients, so you can easily swap or substitute some of the ingredients to suit what you have at home.

MAKES 18 TO 20

9oz fresh or frozen raw peeled shrimp, defrosted if frozen and patted dry with paper towel

vegetable oil, for frying

1 small pack (about 1oz) of fresh cilantro, finely chopped

1 heaped teaspoon garlic granules

finely grated zest of 1 unwaxed lime, the zested lime cut into wedges to serve

1 heaped teaspoon pul biber chile flakes

1 teaspoon cumin seeds

1 egg

2 tablespoons all-purpose flour

1 teaspoon baking powder

5 scallions, thinly sliced diagonally from root to tip

Maldon sea salt flakes and freshly ground black pepper

sweet chilli sauce, to serve

Put the shrimp into a small food processor and briefly pulse until they are chopped but not minced to a paste. Transfer to a small mixing bowl.

Add all the remaining ingredients to the mixing bowl, season very generously with salt and pepper, and stir to combine until evenly mixed together.

Heat a deep skillet over medium-high heat, pour in about 1 inch of vegetable oil, and bring to frying temperature. (Add a pinch of the mixture. If it sizzles immediately, the oil is hot enough.) Line a plate with a double layer of paper towels.

Using 2 teaspoons, form the paste into little quenelles, carefully add to the hot oil, and fry in batches for a minute or so on each side until golden brown. Remove with a slotted spoon and transfer to the paper-lined plate to drain. Enjoy with sweet chill sauce and the lime wedges for squeezing over.

Serve with Warm Harissa, Broccolini & Black Rice Salad (see page 41).

Roasted Vegetable, Za'atar & Labneh Tartines

Good things can be born out of laziness and necessity. Not something Plato would say, but merely one of my own observations from many years spent in the kitchen creating meals that make me happy. This one-pan genius came to me while, you guessed it, recipe testing! I wanted a quick lunch using leftover ingredients and, since I was time poor having already spent a lot cooking, I threw them all onto the same baking pan and hoped for the best. And it worked! This is really very good, and because it's served with bread, it feels substantial and rewarding enough to make a proper meal.

MAKES 4

2 red onions, halved, then each half cut into 3 wedges

1 eggplant, peeled and cut into 1½-inch chunks

garlic oil

3 heaped tablespoons za'atar

5½oz baby plum tomatoes, halved

4 large slices of sourdough bread

1¼ cups labneh or thick Greek yogurt, strained

Maldon sea salt flakes and freshly ground black pepper

Preheat the oven to 425°F. Line your largest baking pan with parchment paper.

Place the onion wedges on one side of the lined pan and break them up a little, then add the eggplant chunks to other side. Drizzle both the onion and eggplant generously with garlic oil and sprinkle each with a heaped tablespoon of za'atar and a generous amount of black pepper. Then use your hands to evenly coat them in the oil and seasonings.

Arrange the tomatoes, cut-side up, on a different part of the pan, sprinkle with 1 heaped teaspoon of za'atar, and season with pepper, but don't add any oil.

Roast for 30 minutes. Remove from the oven, season with salt, and set aside.

Toast the sourdough bread in a toaster, then divide the labneh or yogurt between each slice and top with a portion of the roasted vegetables, plus an extra seasoning using the remaining za'atar if desired. This needs no accompaniment.

Bean & Feta Patties

These lovely little patties are quick and easy to make, and you can serve them in a multitude of ways. I wholeheartedly recommend following the serving suggestion below, but—to give you another simple option—I love serving them as sliders, with mini burger buns, lettuce, and tomato slices on the side. They are also excellent tucked into wraps.

MAKES 12

14oz can cannellini beans, drained and rinsed

1 teaspoon ground turmeric

1 teaspoon pul biber chile flakes

1 teaspoon cumin seeds

4 scallions, thinly sliced from root to tip, 1 reserved for garnish

handful of chopped flat-leaf parsley

⅔ cup crumbled feta cheese

vegetable oil, for frying

Maldon sea salt flakes and freshly ground black pepper

To serve

3 to 4 tablespoons Greek yogurt

3 to 4 tablespoons pomegranate molasses or sweet tamarind sauce

¼ cup pomegranate seeds

Put the beans into a mixing bowl and mash them to a smooth paste. Add the spices, 3 of the scallions, and the parsley and mix together well. Add a very generous seasoning of salt and pepper followed by the feta and gently stir to combine without mashing the feta.

Place a large skillet over medium-high heat and drizzle in enough oil to coat the bottom. Divide the mixture into 12 equal balls (to be as precise as possible, you can weigh the mixture and divide it) and then gently flatten the balls into patties. Once the oil is hot, fry the patties, in batches if necessary, for a couple of minutes on each side until deeply golden brown. Beware that the patties are soft and may break if not handled carefully, so use a spatula to carefully flip them over and then remove them from the skillet.

Serve on a platter drizzled with the yogurt and pomegranate molasses or sweet tamarind sauce, and scattered with the reserved scallion and pomegranate seeds.

Serve with Pan-fried Salmon with Barberry Butter (see page 133).

Halloumi & Avocado Wraps with Harissa Ketchup

I always have halloumi in my refrigerator and I have tried many versions of halloumi sandwiches, from stuffed into pitta breads, on toast, or in burger bunss, but this wrap is one of my favorites. The harissa ketchup really makes this wrap so flavorsome and it is such a quick and comforting lunch or dinner.

MAKES 2

olive oil

9oz block of halloumi cheese, cut into 8 slices

1 tablespoon dried wild oregano

2 large tortilla wraps

1 large tomato, cut in half, then cut into half moons

½ small red onion, cut in half, then thinly sliced into half moons

4 lettuce leaves

1 avocado, halved, stone removed, and cut into slices

3 to 4 tablespoons Greek yogurt

For the harissa ketchup

1 heaped tablespoon harissa

3 tablespoons tomato ketchup

Heat a dry skillet over medium-high heat (medium heat if using a gas stove).

Drizzle a little olive oil on both sides of the halloumi slices. Once the skillet is hot, add the halloumi and fry it for 3 minutes or so on each side until nicely browned and somewhat soft.

Scatter one-quarter of the oregano onto each wrap, then add 4 slices of cooked halloumi to each wrap. Layer the tomato, onion, lettuce, and avocado on top of the halloumi.

Add dollops of yogurt on top of the salad. Then stir the harissa and ketchup to combine, drizzle the mixture over the salad, and scatter with the remaining oregano. Fold up the wraps and serve. This needs no accompaniment.

Sweet Potato & Chickpea Balls

Though they are inspired by my love for falafels, these are quite different and much lighter than the source of their inspiration. Serving them with salad on the side is wonderful, but I also like piling them into wraps with harissa yogurt or into white rolls with some yogurt, mango chutney, and a squeeze of lime juice.

MAKES 18 TO 20

1lb 2oz sweet potatoes, unpeeled

14oz can chickpeas, well drained and patted dry

1 small onion, minced

1 teaspoon ground cumin

1 teaspoon pul biber chile flakes

1 teaspoon ground coriander

½ teaspoon ground cinnamon

2 garlic cloves, minced

3 tablespoons all-purpose flour

1 teaspoon baking powder

½ small pack (about ½oz) of fresh cilantro, very finely chopped

1 tablespoon black and white sesame seeds

1 teaspoon nigella seeds

Maldon sea salt flakes and freshly ground black pepper

pitta breads, to serve

For the harissa yogurt (optional)

⅔ cup Greek or plant-based yogurt

1 tablespoon harissa

Preheat the oven to 400°F. Line a baking pan with parchment paper. Place the sweet potatoes on the lined pan and roast for an hour. Remove from the oven and set aside. When cool enough to handle, peel the skins.

Tip the well drained chickpeas into a large mixing bowl. Using a masher, meat tenderizer, or the end of a rolling pin, mash as finely as possible. Add the peeled sweet-potato flesh, onion, spices, garlic, flour, baking powder, and a generous amount of salt and pepper. Lastly, add the fresh cilantro, and mix together well.

Line your baking pan with fresh parchment paper. Roll the mixture into 18 to 20 balls and arrange on the pan. Mix the sesame seeds with the nigella seeds and scatter over each ball. Let chill in the refrigerator for an hour.

Meanwhile, pour the yogurt into a small bowl (if using) and stir through the harissa just enough to create a marble effect.

When ready to bake, preheat the oven to 425°F. Bake the balls for 12 to 14 minutes until nicely browned. Remove from the oven and let cool for a few minutes so that they firm up slightly, then serve with pitta breads and the harissa yogurt if desired.

Serve with Roasted Eggplants with Spicy Peanut Sauce (see page 173).

Meat, Poultry, Fish & Seafood,

Chicken, Apricot, Orange & Almond Tagine

Tagines are that wonderful marriage of meat or vegetables with sweet and spiced flavor pairings. What you put into yours is entirely up to you and may depend on tradition, local and seasonal availability, and personal preference, of course. I like my tagines to have lots of texture and layers of deep flavor, not just from meat but also from dried fruits, nuts, and fresh herbs. This particular combination can perhaps be called the sweeter cousin of the classic chicken, olive, and preserved lemon, turning away from the wonderfully sour character of the lemon to the more gently acidic profile of orange and that irresistible, almost syrupy, sweet chewiness of dried apricots, plumped from absorbing the broth of the tagine.

SERVES 6 TO 8

vegetable oil

2 large onions, coarsely chopped

2¼lb bone-in, skinless chicken thighs

6 fat garlic cloves, thinly sliced

1 heaped teaspoon cumin seeds

1 teaspoon ground cinnamon

1 teaspoon paprika

1 teaspoon ground ginger

½ teaspoon cayenne pepper

finely grated zest and juice of
   1 unwaxed orange

1 tablespoon honey

¾ cup dried apricots

⅓ cup whole blanched almonds

Maldon sea salt flakes and freshly
   ground black pepper

½ small pack (about ½oz) of flat-leaf
   parsley, leaves coarsely chopped,
   to garnish

Place a large saucepan over medium-high heat, add a drizzle of vegetable oil, and fry the onions until softened and translucent. Add the chicken thighs and garlic and stir well. Mix in the spices, stir, and cook for a few minutes before adding the orange zest and juice, honey, and a generous amount of salt and pepper. Cook for a further 5 minutes, stirring occasionally.

Add enough boiling water to just about cover the ingredients, reduce to a low-medium heat, and cook, uncovered, for 1½ hours, stirring occasionally. Stir in the dried apricots and cook for a further 30 minutes.

Meanwhile, preheat the oven to 425°F. Spread the almonds out on a baking pan and toast for 8 minutes. Remove from the oven and let cool.

When the tagine is ready, serve scattered with the toasted almonds and parsley.

Serve with Cheat's Zereshk Polow (see page 195).

Herb Koftas with Warm Yogurt Sauce & Spiced Mint Butter

While this isn't a Turkish recipe, a lot of what I create is inspired by flavors and techniques used in Turkish, Persian, and Middle Eastern cuisines. I prefer to make smallish meatballs for this recipe, but you can make them bigger if you like. These are lovely served with small pasta shapes, such as orzo, or rice or pillowy bread.

MAKES 35 TO 40
MEATBALLS
SERVES 4 TO 6

1lb 2oz ground lamb

6 scallions, thinly sliced from root to tip, 2 reserved for garnish

2 fat garlic cloves, minced

1 heaped teaspoon pul biber chile flakes

1 heaped teaspoon paprika

1 heaped teaspoon dried mint

1 small pack (about 1oz) of flat-leaf parsley, finely chopped, some reserved for garnish

1 small pack (about 1oz) of dill, finely chopped, some reserved for garnish

½ teaspoon baking soda

vegetable oil, for frying

1 cup Greek yogurt

Maldon sea salt flakes and freshly ground black pepper

For the butter

½ stick butter

1 teaspoon dried mint

1 teaspoon pul biber chile flakes

Put the ground lamb, scallions, garlic, spices, dried mint, fresh herbs, and baking soda into a mixing bowl and season very generously with salt and pepper. Use your hands to work the ingredients together really well until you have an evenly combined smooth paste, then roll the mixture into 35 to 40 balls.

Heat a drizzle of oil in a large skillet over medium-high heat. Line a plate with a double layer of paper towels. Once the pan is hot, add the meatballs and fry on one side for 3 to 4 minutes, then turn and fry on the other side for 3 to 4 minutes before shaking the pan to finish frying the other sides.

Meanwhile, put the yogurt into a saucepan, season with salt and pepper, and heat gently (to stop it from curdling) until hot, then remove from the heat.

Melt the butter with the dried mint and pul biber in a small saucepan.

Once the meatballs are cooked, transfer to the paper-lined plate to drain, then place them on a platter. Drizzle with the yogurt and the butter. Scatter with the reserved scallions and chopped herbs to serve.

Serve with Tomato & Feta Fritters (see page 181).

Dried Lime & Spice-Marinated Lamb Chops

It seems few cultures embrace sour flavorings quite the way we Persians and some Arabs do. Dried white limes are funny little things. To the untrained eye, these wrinkled, ugly little dried-up limes look like they need throwing away. But as you'll discover, they possess a wealth of flavor and a marvelous acidity that can be used in many dishes in different ways. I must admit that I was an adult before I first saw dried black limes—and I was shocked! We Persians don't tend to use them, but now I buy them when I can to either prick and then add them stews whole or—better still—crush and grind them to make a spectacular souring agent that can be added to everything from soups and stews to marinades and cocktails. Here they bring a citrus kick that's absolutely wonderful with lamb.

SERVES 2

3 dried limes (white or black)

1 teaspoon cumin seeds, toasted in a dry pan for 1 to 2 minutes

2 teaspoons garlic granules

1 teaspoon paprika

3 tablespoons olive oil

juice of ½ lime

4 lamb chops

Maldon sea salt flakes and freshly ground black pepper

To serve

steamed white rice

chopped tomatoes

finely sliced red onion

chopped parsley leaves

Preheat your oven to its highest setting. Line a roasting pan with parchment paper.

Put the dried limes and toasted cumin seeds into a spice grinder or bullet blender and blitz together until finely ground to a powder, or use a mortar and pestle. Transfer to a mixing bowl, add all the remaining ingredients, except the lamb, and season well with salt and pepper. Mix into a paste, then rub the paste all over both sides of the lamb chops.

Place the lamb chops on the lined roasting pan and roast for 14 to 16 minutes (depending how high your oven temperature reaches and the thickness of the lamb) until cooked through to your liking. Remove from the oven and serve immediately with plain white rice and a tomato, onion, and parsley salad.

Serve with Oven-baked Spicy Chickpeas & Eggplants with Yogurt & Herbs (see page 174) or Dampokhtak (see page 196).

Lamb, Dried Fig & Preserved Lemon Tagine

Box-ticking all the crucial elements I love in a good tagine, this flavorsome combination, though not authentic, marries together sweet, sour, spicy, and crunchy components. I prefer lamb neck, but boneless lamb shoulder is another option, if you prefer. The warm spices in tagines are a flavor explosion and, while often sweet, there is always a contrasting sharp element that creates perfect balance. Here, preserved lemons come into play and, for a fruitier burst of sharpness, I've added barberries. Hazelnuts provide the crunch.

SERVES 6 TO 8

olive oil

2 large onions, coarsely chopped

1¾lb lamb neck or boneless shoulder, cut into 1-inch chunks

1 bulb of garlic, cloves separated, peeled and kept whole

1 heaped teaspoon ground cumin

1 teaspoon ground cinnamon

1 teaspoon ground turmeric

2 tablespoons honey

2 cups dried figs, some whole, some halved

2 tablespoons dried barberries

4 preserved lemons, seeded and each cut into 3 to 4 thick slices

⅓ cup blanched hazelnuts, chopped

Maldon sea salt flakes and freshly ground black pepper

½ small pack (about ½oz) of flat-leaf parsley, coarsely chopped, to garnish

Place a large saucepan over medium-high heat, add a drizzle of olive oil, and fry the onions until softened and translucent. Add the lamb and garlic cloves and stir well. Mix in the spices, stir, and cook for a few minutes before adding the honey and a generous amount of salt and pepper. Mix well, then cook for a further 10 to 15 minutes, stirring occasionally.

Add enough boiling water to just about cover the ingredients, reduce to low-medium heat, and cook, uncovered, for 1½ hours, stirring occasionally.

Stir in the figs, barberries, and preserved lemons and cook for a further 30 minutes.

Meanwhile, preheat the oven to 425°F. Spread the hazelnuts out on a baking pan and toast for 8 minutes. Check them after 6 minutes to ensure they do not burn. Remove from the oven, let cool, then coarsely chop.

Taste and adjust the seasoning of the tagine if desired, scatter with the parsley and hazelnuts, and serve.

Serve with Cheat's Zereshk Polow (see page 195).

My Tender TFC

Turmeric colors this chicken to match the famous yellow-tinged fried chicken of Malaysia, but the buttermilk has been borrowed from the Americans as a tenderizer. Buttered corn on the cob makes a perfect accompaniment.

SERVES 4 TO 6

2¼lb bone-in, skin-on chicken thighs
 and drumsticks
vegetable oil, for deep-frying
Maldon sea salt flakes and freshly
 ground black pepper
4 to 6 cobs of corn, cooked, to serve
 (optional)

For the coating
1¾ cups all-purpose flour
3 tablespoons ground turmeric
1 tablespoon garlic granules
½ teaspoon cayenne pepper

For the marinade
1¼ cups buttermilk
1 tablespoon ground turmeric
1 tablespoon garlic granules
1 teaspoon paprika
1 teaspoon coriander
½ teaspoon cayenne pepper

Mix the marinade ingredients together in a large mixing bowl. Add the chicken and a generous amount of salt and pepper, then use your hands to mix everything together well and to ensure the chicken is evenly coated all over. Cover the bowl with plastic wrap and let marinate in the refrigerator for at least 4 hours or overnight.

When you are ready to fry, mix the coating ingredients and a generous amount of salt and pepper together in another bowl.

Heat a large, deep saucepan over medium-high heat, pour in about 3 inches of vegetable oil, and bring to frying temperature. (Add a breadcrumb. If it sizzles immediately, the oil is hot enough.) Put a double layer of paper towels on a large plate and set aside.

Using tongs, take a piece of chicken out of the marinade, roll it in the coating mixture until well coated and carefully lower into the hot oil. Fry the chicken in batches for 15 to 20 minutes, or until the chicken is crisp and nicely golden brown and cooked through. Remove from the pan and let drain on the paper towels while you cook the second batch. Let stand for a minute or two before serving with corn on the cob if desired.

Serve with Curried Potato Salad (see page 38) or Warm Orzo, Black-eyed Pea & Herb Salad (see page 42).

My Ultimate Ground Beef & Eggplant

The combination of ground beef and eggplant is popular in so many cuisines in the East and for good reason—it's an absolute winner! This is the perfect dish to serve with just some flatbread on the side, because it has everything you could possibly want already. While you could bake the eggplant if you prefer—after brushing with the spiced oil, bake on a parchment paper-lined baking pan for 25 to 30 minutes in the oven preheated to 400°F—frying does make them more supple and delicious. Your choice! I am all for making my recipes fit in with your preferences, but just be sure to try this one because it is the perfect dish.

SERVES 2 TO 4

1 teaspoon paprika

1 teaspoon ground cumin

¼ cup garlic oil

1 large eggplant, cut into slices about
    ½ inch in thickness (about 8 to 9)

For the topping

9oz ground beef

1 heaped tablespoon rose harissa

1 teaspoon garlic granules

⅔ cup Greek yogurt

handful of chopped flat-leaf parsley

pomegranate molasses, for drizzling

Maldon sea salt flakes

Heat a large skillet over medium heat. Mix the spices with the garlic oil, then brush both sides of the eggplant slices with the spiced oil. Once the pan is hot, add the eggplant slices and cook for 8 minutes or so on each side until soft and deeply browned. Remove from the pan and set aside covered loosely with aluminum foil to keep warm.

Increase the heat under the skillet to high, add the ground beef along with the harissa, garlic granules, and a good seasoning of salt. Immediately break up the beef as finely as you can to prevent it from cooking in clumps. Continue cooking the ground beef, stirring as you go, until brown and fully cooked.

Arrange the eggplant slices on a serving platter and top and surround with the the ground beef, then dollop with the yogurt, scatter with the parsley, and drizzle with pomegranate molasses. Serve immediately.

Serve with Beet & Pomegranate Salad (see page 13) or Spice-roasted Potatoes with Bell Pepper, Tomato & Harissa Sauce (see page 166).

Ground Lamb Börek

My first trip to Turkey was more than 20 years ago, visiting my best friend Aysegul and her family in Istanbul. I remember 12 Turkish women in the family gathered to show me different recipes, beginning with choosing the right meat at the butchers and how to cut and grind it, to the techniques for rolling stuffed leaves and layering börek. It was an experience I will cherish. This recipe is based on the traditional Turkish *kıymalı börek*. I've using filo instead of the traditional (often homemade) *yufka* pastry and a little sprinkle of nigella seeds. I always say go big or go home, so this recipe also provides a more generous filling.

SERVES 7 TO 9

1lb 2oz ground lamb (20% fat)

vegetable oil

1 large onion, very finely chopped

½ stick butter, melted

8 sheets of filo pastry

3 tablespoons milk

pinch of nigella seeds

Maldon sea salt flakes and
  freshly ground black pepper

Remove the ground lamb from the refrigerator 30 minutes before cooking to come up to room temperature.

Preheat the oven to 425°F. Select a 10-inch round ovenproof dish (or anything of similar volume, whether square or rectangular).

Place a skillet over medium heat, drizzle in some vegetable oil, and fry the onion until soft and translucent but without coloring. Add the ground lamb and immediately break it up as finely as possible to prevent it from cooking in clumps to ensure it will spread evenly in the börek. Don't brown the meat or cook it over high heat because you want it to remain soft and tender in every bite. Continue cooking the lamb, stirring as you go, until fully cooked, then season generously with salt and pepper, stir well, and set aside.

Brush the bottom of your ovenproof dish with melted butter. Arrange 2 filo pastry sheets in the dish overlapping if necessary so they completely cover the bottom and sides, then brush with melted butter. Divide the ground lamb into 3 equal portions and spread one portion evenly on the filo base. Cover with another 2 filo pastry sheets and generously brush them with milk so they are visibly wet. Repeat the layering of lamb and filo pastry sheets brushed with milk until you reach the final layer of lamb. Fold the loose edges of filo over the lamb, then arrange the final 2 filo pastry sheets on top, overlapping if necessary so they cover the lamb. Brush the remaining butter over all the pastry and sides, then tuck the edges down inside the dish.

Sprinkle with the nigella seeds and bake for 25 minutes or until nicely golden on top, then serve.

Serve with Burnt Zucchini with Lemon & Feta Yogurt (see page 145) or Mama Ghanoush (see page 158).

Crispy Sticky Lamb with Harissa

Cantonese crispy shredded beef with chiles is one of my all-time favorite dishes. This is very much my own creation and my nod to that wonderful combination of sweet and sticky, crispy and chewy bites of meat but using lamb and adding bell peppers to the mixture instead of carrots. It's an explosion of flavor that ticks every box.

SERVES 3 TO 4

⅓ cup cornstarch

¾lb lamb leg steaks, cut into strips ½ inch in thickness

vegetable oil, for frying

1 large onion, halved and thinly sliced into half moons

1 red bell pepper, cored, seeded, and cut into very thin strips

5 scallions, thinly sliced from root to tip, reserve some for garnish

Maldon sea salt flakes and freshly ground black pepper

steamed white rice, to serve

For the sauce

⅓ cup honey

¼ cup rose harissa

3 tablespoons rice vinegar

2 tablespoons light soy sauce

2 tablespoons cornstarch

Mix the cornstarch with a very generous amount of salt and pepper in a mixing bowl, add the strips of lamb, and really work the cornstarch into the meat for a minute or so. Set aside.

Heat a large skillet over medium-high heat, pour in about 1 inch of vegetable oil and bring to frying temperature. (Add a small piece of a lamb strip. If it sizzles immediately, the oil is hot enough.) Line a plate with a double layer of paper towels.

While the oil is heating up, place a small saucepan over medium heat, add all the sauce ingredients, and whisk together until no lumps of cornstarch remain and the mixture is smooth. Heat the sauce through but do not let it bubble or burn, then remove from the heat.

Fry the lamb strips in batches in the hot oil for about 2 to 3 minutes, or until very crisp on the outside. Remove with a slotted spoon and transfer to the paper-lined plate to drain.

Heat another large skillet over high heat, add a drizzle of vegetable oil, and stir-fry the onion and red bell pepper until browned a little. Add the lamb strips followed by the sauce and toss together until evenly coated, then add the scallions and stir to combine well. Serve immediately, scattered with the reserved scallions and alongside steamed white rice. This needs no accompaniment.

Nargessi Kofta Loaf

Nargessi kofta is the recipe from which the British Scotch egg may well have been derived. Fortnum & Mason department store in London claims to have created the Scotch egg in 1738 as a picnic food, but its origins are likely to have been in dishes experienced by the British during their time in India. Even further back than this, the recipe is thought to have been brought to India by Persian cooks who came to the Mughal courts. Essentially, it's a kofta. This is my version, inspired by the flavors of Persia, and containing whole hard-cooked eggs. This is a wonderfully juicy meatloaf recipe unlike any other.

SERVES 4 TO 6

4 eggs, divided

1lb 2oz ground lamb

1 large onion, very finely chopped

½ cup dried apricots, each cut into
    4 or 5 strips

⅓ cup pistachio nuts, coarsely
    chopped

2 tablespoons dried barberries

2 tablespoons tomato paste

1 teaspoon baking soda

1 teaspoon ground turmeric

2 teaspoons garlic granules

½ small pack (about ½oz) of flat-leaf
    parsley, finely chopped

½ small pack (about ½oz) of fresh
    cilantro, finely chopped

Maldon sea salt flakes and freshly
    ground black pepper

Preheat the oven to 350°F. Line the bottom of a 2-pound (9-inch) loaf pan with parchment paper.

Cook 3 of the eggs in a small saucepan of boiling water for 6 minutes, then drain and place under cold running water to cool. When cool enough to handle, peel off the shells and set the eggs aside.

Put all the remaining ingredients, including the other egg (to bind) and a generous amount of salt and pepper, into a mixing bowl and use your hands to work the ingredients together really well for a couple of minutes until you have an evenly combined paste.

Divide the mixture in half and place the first half in the pan. Arrange the boiled eggs lengthwise down the center and then lay the rest of the mixture on top, being extra gentle so that you don't burst the eggs. Smooth the surface and make sure it is completely sealed. Bake for 40 minutes.

Remove the loaf from the oven and let stand for 5 minutes. Then, using a nonmetallic utensil such as a spatula to ensure the edges come out cleanly, invert the loaf onto a large plate, cut into slices, and serve.

Serve with Roasted Vegetable & Mixed Bean Salad with Herb Dressing (see page 33) or Warm Orzo, Black-eyed Pea & Herb Salad (see page 42).

Ras el Hanout, Orange & Lamb Rib Chop Platter

Rib chops would be the cut of lamb (my favorite meat) that I would go for if I had to choose just one. They have the perfect amount of fat and bone and a wonderful eye of meat, which makes their proportions ideal for marinating, broiling, barbecuing, and roasting. This is very much a complete meal of a recipe that needs little else. It feels almost celebratory, but don't let that stop you from enjoying it whenever you like. The spiced components when brought together create a real explosion of flavor that you'll want to experience again and again.

SERVES 3 TO 4

8 to 10 well-trimmed lamb rib chops

3 to 4 tablespoons garlic oil

2 tablespoons ras el hanout

finely grated zest of 1 unwaxed orange and juice of ½

Maldon sea salt flakes and freshly ground black pepper

For the potatoes

3¼lb potatoes, peeled and cut into about 1½-inch chunks

3 tablespoons ghee (or vegetable oil if you prefer)

8 fat garlic cloves, thinly sliced

2 tablespoons dried fenugreek leaves

2 teaspoons cumin seeds

2 teaspoons ground turmeric

1 teaspoon dried red chile flakes (omit if you prefer)

½ cup cold water

1 small pack (about 1oz) of flat-leaf parsley, leaves coarsely chopped

For the eggplants

3 small or 2 large eggplants, peeled, halved lengthwise ,and cut into coarse 1¼-inch chunks

about 5 to 6 tablespoons garlic oil

2 teaspoons paprika

To serve

1 cup Greek yogurt

sweet tamarind sauce, for drizzling

½ cup pistachio slivers (or very coarsely chopped whole nuts)

⅓ cup pomegranate seeds

continued overleaf

Put the lamb rib chops into a shallow bowl or dish, add the garlic oil, ras el hanout, orange zest and juice, and a generous amount of salt, then rub the mixture evenly all over the rib chops. Cover the bowl or dish with plastic wrap and let marinate at room temperature while you cook the eggplants and potatoes.

Preheat the oven to 425°F. Line your largest baking pan with parchment paper.

Place the eggplant chunks on the lined pan and drizzle with the garlic oil. Sprinkle with the paprika and a good amount of salt, then use your hands to evenly coat the chunks in the oil and spice. Arrange in a single layer on the lined pan and place in the oven for about 25 minutes until nicely browned and starting to char around the edges. Remove from the oven and set aside.

Meanwhile, parboil the potatoes in a saucepan of boiling water for 10 minutes, then tip into a colander to drain. Return the saucepan to low-medium heat, add the ghee (or vegetable oil), garlic slices, fenugreek leaves, and spices. Fry for a few minutes, ensuring they don't burn. Pour in the water and stir, then add the parboiled potatoes with a generous amount of salt and pepper. Mix together until evenly coated in the spices and garlic. Cover the pan with a lid and cook gently for about 20 minutes, stirring occasionally to prevent the ingredients from sticking.

Place the eggplants back in the oven to reheat gently. Then check the potatoes, which should be a little browned when done and cooked through. Stir through the chopped parsley, reserving a little for a garnish.

Heat a skillet over medium-high heat and cook the marinated lamb rib chops for 2 to 3 minutes on each side. Remove from the pan and let rest while you get ready to serve.

Transfer the potatoes to a very large serving platter, then add the eggplants and scatter with the remaining parsley. Arrange the lamb rib chops on top. Lastly, dollop with the yogurt, drizzle with sweet tamarind sauce, and finish with the pistachios and pomegranate seeds. This needs no accompaniment.

Persian Dolmeh-e barg

This recipe from my childhood is very dear to my heart, but not having the original recipe, I taught myself and experimented for many years to get it right so that the flavors matched my memories. *Dolmeh* is the Persian word for dolma, and we Persians eat the same filling in both stuffed vine leaves (*barg e moo*) as well as in onions, tomatoes, bell peppers, and cabbage leaves. Rather than cigar shapes, our *dolmeh* are fashioned to look almost like plump teabags, which I think makes them infinitely less fiddly and a lot more substantial and satisfying. They are traditionally cooked on a stove, but I have found that baking ensures they cook through evenly. If you can, make them the day before eating. They really do benefit from resting overnight and refrigeration, and a gentle reheating the next day.

MAKES 25 TO 30

vegetable oil

1 large onion, finely chopped

9oz ground lamb

1 small pack (about 1oz) of fresh cilantro, finely chopped

1 small pack (about 1oz) of flat-leaf parsley, finely chopped

1 small pack (about 1oz) of chives, thinly sliced

3 tablespoons dried dill

1 teaspoon ground turmeric

¼ cup uncooked yellow split peas

1 cup basmati rice

1 bunch of scallions, thinly sliced from root to tip

1 pack or jar of vine leaves in brine, drained

Maldon sea salt flakes and freshly ground black pepper

For the tomato liquid

2 cups boiling water

⅓ cup superfine sugar

2 heaped tablespoons tomato paste

juice of 1 lemon

1 tablespoon olive oil

continued overleaf

Pour all the ingredients for the tomato liquid into a small pitcher, stir together until the sugar has dissolved, and then set aside.

Place a large skillet over medium-high heat, drizzle in some vegetable oil, and fry the onion until soft and translucent. Add the ground lamb along with all the herbs, turmeric, and a generous amount of salt and pepper and immediately break it up as finely as you can to prevent it from cooking in clumps. Then add the split peas, rice, and scallions and cook gently for 10 to 15 minutes, stirring gently so as not to break the rice grains. Remove from the heat and let cool completely.

Preheat the oven to 350°F.

Place a dessertspoonful of the meat filling on a vine leaf and roll up into a little fat parcel shape, about the size of a teabag. How you roll or seal the parcels really doesn't matter, and broken leaves can always be overlaid with another leaf. Repeat until all the meat filling is used up.

Take a large ovenproof dish and line the bottom with vine leaves (if you don't have enough, use a double layer of aluminum foil or parchment paper). Arrange the dolmeh, seam-side down and tightly packed, in the lined dish, then pour over the tomato liquid, and cover with a double layer of foil. Bake for 2 hours, then remove the foil and bake for a further 30 minutes. Remove from the oven and let cool. These are best made the day before eating to allow the flavors to intensify, so refrigerate them until you are ready to serve the next day.

To reheat the dolmeh, preheat the oven to 350°F and take the dolmeh out of the fridge. Lift the foil covering, add a splash of water, then replace the foil. Place in the oven to reheat for 20 to 25 minutes, or until warmed through. These are best eaten warm rather than piping hot.

Serve with Burnt Zucchini with Lemon & Feta Yogurt (see page 145) or Roasted Tomatoes with Labneh & Sumac Spice Oil (see page 177).

Spiced Lamb & Potato Stew

I absolutely love Massamun (meaning "Muslim") curry, a recipe thought to have Persian roots, thanks to Persian traders bringing influences and ingredients of their own on their travels to South East Asia. While this recipe is not remotely like a Massamun curry, it does include many of the same comforting notes and flavors, and can easily be recreated at home and all in one pot. For me, the combination of sweet and spice works so well in curries and stews that I find it incredibly hard to resist. You can also substitute beef shin for the lamb if you like. I like to serve this with plain boiled rice or bread.

SERVES 6

3 tablespoons vegetable oil

2 onions, halved and thinly sliced into half moons

1 tablespoon cumin seeds

1 tablespoon ground cumin

2 black cardamom pods

1 tablespoon ground cinnamon

1 teaspoon ground turmeric

½ teaspoon dried red chile flakes

2 star anise

2 tablespoons superfine sugar

2 tablespoons rose harissa

1¾lb boneless lamb shoulder, cut into 1-inch cubes

6 fat garlic cloves, peeled and kept whole

1lb 2oz baby new potatoes

14fl oz can coconut milk

2 handfuls of salted peanuts

Maldon sea salt flakes and freshly ground black pepper

plain boiled rice or bread to serve

Place a large saucepan over medium-high heat, add the vegetable oil, and fry the onions until soft and beginning to brown. Add all the spices, sugar, and rose harissa and mix really well until evenly combined. Cook for a few minutes, stirring regularly to prevent it from burning.

Add the lamb and garlic cloves along with a generous amount of salt and pepper and stir to coat the meat in the onion and spice mixture, then let it cook for a few minutes. Add enough boiling water to almost cover the ingredients, stir the contents of the pan again, and reduce to medium heat. Cover the pan with a lid and cook for 2 hours, stirring occasionally to prevent the mixture from sticking.

Remove the lid, stir again, and mix in the potatoes and coconut milk, then cook, uncovered, for a further hour. Check the amount of liquid and add a little more water if needed (it should be a rich sauce, but not watery). Taste and adjust the seasoning, if desired, then serve with the peanuts scattered on top. Serve with rice or bread. This needs no accompaniment.

Torsh,e Shami

These little shamis came into my life when I was kid. I remember tasting them thinking they were the usual Persian shamis (a simple unspiced patty of mashed chickpeas and lamb with a hole poked through the center). At first bite I had the shock of my life! They were spicy and salty, then this insane burst of sour hit and, well, I was completely hooked. The word *torsh* means "sour" in Persian. They are unlike anything I've ever tasted, and to this day they hold a special place in my heart. This recipe is more Iraqi than Persian, since my grandmother's sister (my grandaunt) was married to an Iraqi and I grew up eating food from both cuisines. These are great with pitta breads or flatbreads and some plain yogurt on the side.

MAKES ABOUT 16

14oz can chickpeas, drained and dried

9oz ground lamb

1 heaped teaspoon ground turmeric

1 teaspoon ground cumin

½ teaspoon ground cinnamon

½ teaspoon cayenne pepper

½ small packet (about ½oz) of flat-leaf parsley, finely chopped

⅓ cup all-purpose flour, divided

1 lemon, peeled, seeded, and flesh finely chopped

1 onion, minced in a food processor or by hand

⅔ cup well dried, finely crumbled feta cheese

vegetable oil, for frying

Maldon sea salt flakes and freshly ground black pepper

To serve

plain yogurt

pitta bread or flatbread

Put the chickpeas, ground lamb, spices, and a generous amount of salt and pepper into a food processor and blitz to a paste. Transfer to a mixing bowl and add the parsley, half the flour, the lemon, onion, and feta (ensuring the latter 3 ingredients are as dry as possible) along with a little more seasoning. Then use your hands to work the ingredients together really well until you have an evenly combined paste.

Divide the mixture into approximately 16 portions and pat each portion into a small patty shape. Lightly dust each side with the remaining flour.

Heat a large skillet over medium-high heat and drizzle in enough vegetable oil to generously coat the bottom. Once hot (but not smoking), fry the patties for a couple of minutes on each side until nicely browned, then serve with yogurt and pitta breads or flatbread.

Serve with Aegean Giant Couscous Salad (see page 10) or My Platter of Dreams (see page 21).

Ras el Hanout Sticky Spatchcock Squab

I am constantly raiding my store cupboards to bolster the flavor in things I cook. This recipe uses that wonderfully aromatic and intense spice blend known as ras el hanout, along with quince paste or jelly (either is suitable) or apricot jam to give a gratifyingly sticky finish. Now the only thing you really might find difficult is to decide whether to be sensible and have just half a squab each or to go the whole hog (or bird!) and enjoy an entire squab yourself.

SERVES 2 TO 4

2 whole squab

olive oil

2 teaspoons ras el hanout

2 tablespoons quince paste or jelly, or apricot jam

Maldon sea salt flakes

Preheat the oven to 425°F. Line a roasting pan with parchment paper.

To spatchcock a squab, place it breast-side down on a cutting board. Using a good sturdy pair of kitchen scissors, cut down either side of the backbone and then remove the bone. Turn the squab over breast-side up and gently press down on it with both hands to flatten it as best you can.

Place the squab, with space between them, on the lined pan. Drizzle each generously with olive oil and sprinkle with the ras el hanout. Then use your hands to rub the oil and spice mix all over the skin of each squab. Season generously with salt and roast for 30 minutes.

Remove from the oven, brush the quince jelly or apricot jam over the top of the squabs and roast for a further 10 minutes until cooked through. Remove from the oven, cover loosely with a piece of aluminum foil, and let the birds rest for 10 minutes before serving.

Serve with Spice-roasted Butternut & Black Rice Salad (see page 30) or Cheat's Zereshk Polow (see page 195).

Taas Kabáb

A *taas kabab* is something entirely different from the meat and vegetables on a skewer you might have been expecting to see when you read this recipe title. In fact, it is a Persian recipe of Turkish descent, which we have adapted by layering meat and vegetables to create a very flavorful and comforting meal. Every Persian household may argue (as they often do) that their version is different, but this is the recipe I know from my childhood when I watched my grandaunt build the layers before slow-cooking this dish. I guess it is essentially what we in the West call a hotpot and therefore not so unfamiliar after all. It's very subtly spiced and really delicious, and a hearty recommendation for the colder months.

SERVES 6 TO 8

vegetable oil

2 large onions, coarsely chopped

1 large bulb of garlic, cloves separated, peeled, and kept whole

1¾lb lamb neck, cut into ½-inch chunks

2 teaspoons ground turmeric

½ teaspoon ground cinnamon

⅓ cup tomato paste

5 carrots, peeled and cut into 1¼-inch chunks

1lb 2oz new potatoes, cut into ½-inch slices (halved if small or cut into 3 slices if larger)

6 large tomatoes, halved horizontally

about 1 cup water

Maldon sea salt flakes and freshly ground pepper

Greek yogurt, to serve

Place a large saucepan with a lid (or a Dutch oven) over medium heat, drizzle in enough vegetable oil to coat the bottom, and fry the onions until softened and translucent. Stir in the garlic cloves. Add the lamb, spices, tomato paste, and a generous amount of salt and pepper and mix to coat the lamb well. Cook for 10 to 15 minutes, stirring occasionally.

Arrange the carrots in a layer over the lamb mixture, then the potatoes, adding a little extra seasoning to the potato layer, and finally top with the tomatoes. Add the water, then place the lid on the pan and cook for 30 minutes over very low heat without stirring.

Remove the lid and, without stirring, gently shake the pan a little and ensure it has some liquid still left in it. Replace the lid and continue cooking the stew gently, reducing the heat more if necessary, for a further 1½ hours. Carefully remove the ingredients from the pan to serve, with yogurt on the side. This needs no accompaniment, but you can always serve it with bread or steamed basmati rice.

Butterflied Lamb with, Tahini Garlic Yogurt

Tender, juicy, and ever so versatile, lamb is my favorite meat of all time. But while I love the gentle, slow-cooked, pull-apart approach of roast leg of lamb, I don't always have the time. So, I choose a butterflied leg of lamb for the ultimate quick-cook convenience. How you serve this beauty is up to you. Sometimes I want it with roast potatoes and other times with rice, bulgur wheat, or couscous, but I can easily be persuaded to slice it as thinly as possible and pile it into pitta breads with sliced onions, tomatoes, and pickles, too.

SERVES 4 TO 6

2¼ to 3¼lb butterflied leg of lamb

3 tablespoons plain yogurt

3 fat garlic cloves, minced

2 teaspoons paprika

2 teaspoons ground cumin

2 teaspoons ground coriander

1 teaspoon ground cinnamon

juice of ½ lemon

2 tablespoons olive oil, plus extra for frying

Maldon sea salt flakes and freshly ground black pepper

For the tahini garlic yogurt

⅔ cup Greek yogurt

⅓ cup tahini

1 garlic clove, minced

good squeeze of lemon juice

To serve

4 to 6 tomatoes, quartered

sliced red onion

flatbreads

Remove the lamb from the refrigerator 20 minutes before you intend to marinate it and ensure it is splayed open and as flat as possible so that the meat cooks evenly. If there are any sides with much thicker meat, use a small sharp knife to make incisions to open them up and flatten as evenly as possible.

For the marinade, stir all the remaining ingredients to combine in a large mixing bowl, seasoning generously with salt and pepper. Place the lamb on a platter and rub the marinade all over, really working it in. Cover with plastic wrap and let marinate for a minimum of 30 minutes at room temperature, or overnight in the refrigerator, if preferred. Remove from the refrigerator 30 minutes or so before cooking to allow the meat to come up to room temperature.

Preheat the oven to 425°F. Line a roasting pan with parchment paper.

continued overleaf

Place a large skillet over medium heat, drizzle in a little olive oil, and once hot, add the marinated lamb to the pan, skin-side down. Seal the lamb until browned on all sides, without letting it blacken or burn. It should have a nice crust in about 10 minutes.

Transfer the lamb to the lined roasting pan and roast for 20 to 25 minutes, depending on how well done you like your meat. I like it very pink and juicy, but if you prefer medium or well done, leave it in the oven for a further 5 to 10 minutes. Once the meat is cooked to your liking, remove from the oven and let rest loosely covered with aluminum foil for 10 to 15 minutes.

Meanwhile, mix the tahini garlic yogurt ingredients together in a bowl and season with salt and pepper, then thin it down to a sauce consistency with some lukewarm water.

Serve the lamb thinly sliced with the tahini garlic yogurt, tomatoes, sliced onion, and flatbreads.

Serve with Spice-roasted Butternut & Black Rice Salad (see page 30), Baked Vegetable & Feta Layers (see page 138), Ras el Hanout & Sweet Potatoes with Tahini Yogurt & Herb Oil (see page 165) or Spice-roasted Potatoes with Bell Pepper, Tomato & Harissa Sauce (see page 166).

Tahchin Two Ways

I shared the most classic tahchin recipe using chicken and barberries with you in my book *Simply*, but I'm delighted to say that there are more versions. Among the most popular are the ground meat tahchin or the eggplant tahchin. Both are delicious. However, I lean toward the meat filling because I do love my meat and the family loves it, too. Having said that, the eggplant filling is a satisfying vegetarian alternative.

SERVES 4 TO 6

2½ cups basmati rice

1¼ cups Greek yogurt

3 large eggs

a small pinch of saffron threads,
    ground to a powder using a mortar
    and pestle, then steeped in ⅓ cup
    boiling water until cool

½ stick butter, melted

melted ghee or vegetable oil,
    for greasing

Maldon sea salt flakes and freshly
    ground black pepper

For the eggplant filling (VEGETARIAN)

3 large eggplants, peeled and cut into
    1-inch cubes

olive oil

1 teaspoon ground cumin

½ teaspoon ground cinnamon

For the meat filling

vegetable oil

1 large onion, finely chopped

1lb 2oz ground lamb

1 teaspoon garlic granules

1 teaspoon ground turmeric

½ teaspoon ground cinnamon

2 tablespoons tomato purée

½ stick butter

4 generous handfuls of frozen peas,
    rinsed in cold water to defrost,
    and then drained

To prepare the eggplant filling
Preheat the oven to 400°F. Line a large baking pan with parchment paper.

Place the eggplant cubes on the lined pan, drizzle generously with olive oil, and rub it in. Season very generously with salt and pepper and the cumin and cinnamon, then use your hands to coat the cubes evenly in the seasoning and spices. Spread out in a single layer and roast for 25 minutes until nicely browned and cooked through. Remove from the oven and set aside.

continued overleaf

To prepare the meat filling

Place a large saucepan over high heat, drizzle in some vegetable oil, and stir-fry the onion until translucent and beginning to turn golden around the edges. Add the ground lamb and immediately break it up as finely as you can to prevent it from cooking in clumps. Add the garlic granules, spices, and tomato paste and stir through to coat the meat and until cooked. Add the butter and a very generous amount of salt and pepper, followed by the peas, then stir until the butter has melted and everything is evenly combined. Taste and adjust the seasoning if desired, then set aside.

To assemble

Bring a large saucepan of water to a boil. Add the rice and stir to stop the grains from sticking together, then parboil for about 6 to 7 minutes until the grains turn from a dullish off-white color to a more opaque, brilliant white and have slightly elongated, though they should still remain firm to the bite. Drain and immediately rinse thoroughly under cold running water, running your fingers through the rice, until all the grains are well rinsed of starch and have completely cooled. Drain the rice thoroughly by shaking the sieve well, then let stand for 10 minutes so any remaining water can drain away. Shake off any excess water before use.

Put the yogurt, eggs, saffron solution, and a generous amount of salt and pepper (bearing in mind that you will need more than you think, since the rice will increase in volume and require more seasoning) into a large mixing bowl and stir until evenly combined. Stir in the parboiled rice, then the melted butter and mix well.

Preheat the oven to 400°F. Line the bottom of a 12 x 8-inch ovenproof dish with parchment paper and brush the paper and sides with melted ghee or vegetable oil. (If you are using a nonstick dish, you can omit the paper and just brush with melted ghee or vegetable oil.)

Pour half the rice mixture into the dish and spread it out. Add your chosen filling on top in an even layer, then cover with the remaining rice mixture and smooth the surface. Bake on the lowest rack in the oven for 80 to 90 minutes, or until the edges are browned.

Once cooked, place a tray or large heatproof platter over the dish and carefully invert the tahchin onto it. Then cut into squares to serve.

Serve the eggplant tahchin with Burnt Zucchini with Lemon & Feta Yogurt (see page 145); serve the meat tahchin with Mama Ghanoush (see page 158).

Tavuk Güveç

My love for Turkish cuisine is well known, and this chicken recipe is another one that just has to be shared. Having published the meat version of *güveç* in my previous book *Persiana Everyday*, I wanted to present this lighter chicken version to you, too. The Turkish pepper paste of the classic recipe can be hard to find, so I have replaced it here with paprika. But should you find a jar, simply substitute it for the paprika to experience the real deal. Either way, this is another one-pot comfort classic that is so delicious it will become a household favorite. I like to serve this with plain boiled rice or bread.

SERVES 6

olive oil

2 large onions, coarsely chopped

2¼lb bone-in, skinless chicken thighs

1 bulb of garlic, cloves separated, peeled, and kept whole

4 bay leaves

1 teaspoon paprika

1 teaspoon pul biber chile flakes

1 teaspoon dried wild oregano

1 teaspoon dried mint

¼ cup tomato paste

1lb 2oz new potatoes, halved

2 red bell peppers, cored, seeded, and cut into big chunks

4 large tomatoes, halved

Maldon sea salt flakes and freshly ground black pepper

Place a large saucepan over medium-high heat, drizzle in some olive oil, and cook the onions until softened and translucent. Stir in the chicken and garlic cloves, then add the bay leaves, spices, dried herbs, tomato paste, and a generous amount of salt and pepper. Cook for 5 minutes, stirring occasionally. Add the potatoes, red bell peppers, and tomatoes and cook for a further 5 minutes.

Add enough boiling water to just about cover the ingredients, reduce the heat to low-medium, and cook uncovered for 2 hours, stirring occasionally. Taste and adjust the seasoning, if desired, then serve. This needs no accompaniment.

The Kids' Chicken Korma

This is one of my kids' favorite dishes I like to cook at home, but don't for a second think that this recipe is just for kids. This is simply a family favorite. "Korma" comes from a Persian term *ghormeh*, meaning "stew," and although this particular recipe bears no resemblance to anything Persian, Indian cuisine has so much influence from Persia. To make it a little more grown up, add ½ to 1 teaspoon dried red chile flakes. Kids generally prefer chicken breast meat, but I prefer chicken thighs, so if that's your preference too, substitute 1¾lb boneless, skinless thigh fillets and cook for 1½ hours instead.

SERVES 4 TO 6

2 to 3 tablespoons vegetable oil
   or ghee
2 large onions, finely chopped
1½lb boneless, skinless chicken
   breasts, split lengthwise and cut
   into ½-inch slices
2 teaspoons medium curry powder
1 heaped teaspoon ground turmeric
½ cup desiccated coconut
¼ cup ground almonds
2 tablespoons superfine sugar
14fl oz can coconut milk
Maldon sea salt flakes and freshly
   ground black pepper
steamed basmati rice, to serve

Heat a medium-sized saucepan over medium heat, add the vegetable oil or ghee, and fry the onions until soft and translucent, but do not let them brown. Add the chicken, spices, coconut, and ground almonds and mix well until evenly combined. Add a generous amount of salt and pepper and then add the sugar. Cook the mixture for 5 to 6 minutes, stirring regularly to prevent any browning or burning.

Pour in the coconut milk and stir until evenly combined (the liquid should mostly cover the chicken). Let the chicken simmer gently, uncovered, for about an hour or so until tender and the sauce is thick enough to coat the back of a spoon. Serve with steamed basmati rice.

Pan-fried Salmon, with Barberry Butter

People always ask me how else they can use barberries at home, and even though I have literally dozens of suggestions, one of the most common answers I give is to make a butter compound out of them along with any herbs and flavors you like, and then use that butter with everything. The lovely citrusy character of barberries means that you can essentially treat them as you would when adding lemon to a dish, but without the bitterness or additional liquid. Here, they provide a wonderful berry sharpness that works so well with the fatty salmon that it really is a perfect pairing.

SERVES 2 TO 4

olive oil

4 skinless salmon fillets,
　　4½ to 5½oz each

Maldon sea salt flakes and freshly
　　ground black pepper

For the barberry butter

⅔ stick butter, softened

2 tablespoons dried barberries,
　　finely chopped

1 teaspoon pul biber chile flakes

1 teaspoon garlic granules

1 tablespoon honey

Put all the barberry butter ingredients into a small bowl, add a good seasoning of salt and pepper, and mix together well. You can use the butter immediately or seal it in plastic wrap and refrigerate for later use.

Heat a large skillet over medium-high heat and drizzle in a little olive oil. Season the salmon fillets on the top surface with salt and pepper, then add, top-side down, to the skillet. Cook for a couple of minutes, then carefully turn them over and immediately add the butter. As soon as the butter melts, begin basting the salmon fillets quickly and repeatedly to prevent the butter from burning, for 2 minutes, or until just cooked through. Serve immediately, drizzled with the butter.

Serve with Nectarine, Halloumi & Cucumber Salad with Cashews (see page 25) or Warm Orzo, Black-eyed Pea & Herb Salad (see page 42).

Spiced & Soupy Seafood Rice

I absolutely love comforting recipes like this for the colder months, especially when seafood is concerned. Admittedly, seafood often feels like a summer thing, but this is really the kind of hearty dish I want to eat when the weather is cold and I need a little warming burst of sunshine to brighten up the darker days. And yes—don't even give it two minutes' thought—serve some crusty bread on the side. It may not be needed, but I feel my whole being benefits from the frequent enjoyment of double carbs, and yours might, too!

SERVES 4 TO 6

olive oil

1 large onion, finely chopped

1 large bulb of garlic, cloves separated, bashed, peeled, and kept whole

1 bay leaf

2 tablespoons harissa

1 tablespoon dried wild oregano

2 large tomatoes, cored and coarsely diced

1 large yellow bell pepper, cored, seeded, and diced

14oz can diced tomatoes

1 teaspoon superfine sugar

1½ quarts cold water

1 cup arborio or carnaroli risotto rice

2¼lb fresh mussels, cleaned

9oz fresh or frozen raw peeled jumbo shrimp, defrosted if frozen

⅔ stick butter, coarsely chopped

½ small pack (about ½oz) of flat-leaf parsley, coarsely chopped, some reserved for garnish

Maldon sea salt flakes and freshly ground black pepper

Place a large saucepan over medium-high heat, drizzle in some olive oil, and cook the onion until softened. Add the garlic cloves and continue cooking until the onion is translucent. Add the bay leaf, harissa, oregano, fresh tomatoes, yellow bell pepper, and a generous amount of salt and pepper and cook, stirring, for a few minutes. Next, add the diced tomatoes and sugar and stir again, then add the water and stir. Reduce to low-medium heat and simmer, uncovered, for 45 minutes.

Add the rice and stir once, then cook for 15 minutes. Taste and adjust the seasoning if desired. Check the liquid volume and add a little hot water if needed, then stir in the mussels, cover again, and cook for 5 minutes until the shells have opened. Stir in the shrimp, cover again, and cook for another minute. Lastly, add the butter with the parsley and stir until melted. Discard any mussels that have not opened, then taste and adjust the seasoning if desired. Serve immediately in shallow bowls and scattered with parsley. This needs no accompaniment other than bread.

Vegetables
& Legumes

Baked Vegetable & Feta Layers

This oven-baked layered vegetable dish requires little effort and doesn't compromise on flavor. I can't recommend this loaf-pan-baked beauty highly enough. I love the oozy dots of feta in it, and the cheese marries so well with the sauce, too.

SERVES 2 TO 4

1 large eggplant, cut into ¼-inch slices

1 large zucchini, cut into ¼-inch slices

olive oil

1 large red bell pepper, cored, seeded, and cut into 6 long strips

2 fat garlic cloves, thinly sliced

½ teaspoon dried red chile flakes

14oz can diced tomatoes

1 teaspoon superfine sugar

7oz feta cheese, broken into small chunks (omit for a vegan option)

Maldon sea salt flakes and freshly ground black pepper

Preheat the oven to 400°F. Line a large baking pan with parchment paper.

Lay the eggplant and zucchini slices on the lined baking pan, brush with olive oil, and season well with salt and pepper. Roast for 35 to 40 minutes. Remove from the oven. Transfer the roasted vegetables to a plate.

Turn your oven up to its highest setting and line the baking pan with fresh parchment paper. Lay the red bell pepper strips, skin-side down, on the lined pan, brush the exposed sides with olive oil, and roast for 15 minutes. Remove from the oven and reduce the oven temperature to 425°F.

To make the sauce, place a small saucepan over medium heat, drizzle in some olive oil, and fry the garlic slices until translucent. Add the dried red chile flakes and stir for a minute before adding the diced tomatoes, sugar, and a good seasoning of salt and pepper. Cook for 20 minutes or so on a gentle simmer, then remove from the heat and blitz with a hand-held stick blender until smooth. Taste and adjust the seasoning if desired.

Pour half the sauce into a 2-pound (9-inch) loaf pan, add a layer of the bell peppers (widthwise or diagonally), then some zucchini, and top with enough of the feta to cover the surface, then add just a little of the sauce. Layer in the remaining vegetables and feta, then cover with the remaining sauce. Carefully press down, then bake for 30 minutes until piping hot. Remove from the oven and let rest for 5 minutes. Then place a plate over the top, carefully invert onto the plate, and serve. Don't worry if it doesn't look neat or collapses. It will still taste sublime.

Serve with Butterflied Lamb with Tahini Garlic Yogurt (see page 123) or Charred Broccoli with Lemons, Chiles, & Yogurt (see page 154).

Bean, Bell Pepper & Thyme Khorak

Khorak is to Persians what a *ragoût* is to the French. Classically it would be a meat braise of some sort, but these days there are many varieties, including one with green beans. As a devoted lover of legumes, there isn't a single variety that I don't love, but rarely do I make them the main dish on a table. This colorful recipe is worthy of centerpiece stardom because it's bright, vibrant, delicious, and really easy to make. As a bonus, you can use any beans you like, which means you'll be more likely to make it time and time again. Enjoy on its own or with rice or crusty bread.

SERVES 4 TO 6

5½oz semi-dried tomatoes in oil, drained and oil reserved

1 large onion, finely chopped

3 large bell peppers (any color, but I like red, orange, and yellow), cored, seeded, and cut into thin strips

6 garlic cloves, thinly sliced

8 to 10 fleshy sprigs of thyme or 3 woody sprigs of thyme, or 1 heaped teaspoon dried thyme

14oz can cannellini beans, drained and rinsed

14oz can red kidney beans, drained and rinsed

14oz can diced tomatoes

1 teaspoon pul biber chile flakes

Maldon sea salt flakes and freshly ground black pepper

crusty bread, to serve

Place a large, deep skillet or shallow saucepan over medium-high heat, drizzle in some of the oil from the semi-dried tomatoes, and fry the onion until beginning to brown around the edges. Add the bell peppers and stir-fry with the onion until they are completely softened and also beginning to brown around the edges.

Next, add the garlic slices, thyme (discarding any woody stalks), cannellini and kidney beans, diced tomatoes, pul biber, and a very generous amount of salt and pepper. Stir well and cook over medium-high heat for 15 to 20 minutes, stirring occasionally to stop the mixture from sticking. Lastly, add the semi-dried tomatoes, taste, and adjust the seasoning if desired. Cook for a further 10 to 15 minutes before serving with crusty bread.

Serve with Cabbage "Bowl" Dolma (see page 147) or Oven-baked Spicy Chickpeas & Eggplants with Yogurt & Herbs (see page 174).

Smoked Eggplants with Lime & Maple Dressing

This is a wonderful way to enjoy eggplants with less traditional flavors than the usual Middle Eastern offering. Even my ordinarily eggplant-shy husband ate more than his fair share of this, making me determined to let you in on the recipe by including it in a book one day. And so, here we are. I hope you love it.

SERVES 2 TO 4

2 large eggplants

4 scallions, thinly sliced diagonally from root to tip

½ small pack (about ½oz) of fresh cilantro, finely chopped

½ teaspoon pul biber chile flakes, or more to taste

generous handful of salted peanuts, coarsely chopped

For the dressing

2 tablespoons olive oil

1 heaped tablespoon maple syrup

finely grated zest and juice of 1 fat unwaxed lime

Maldon sea salt flakes and freshly ground black pepper

Smoke the eggplants whole over an open flame. You can use either a barbecue or a gas stove, using long-handled tongs to continually turn them, until the skin has crackled and become ashen all over, the eggplants have collapsed by half, and the flesh is completely soft on the inside. Remove from the heat and let the eggplants cool until you can handle them.

Mix the dressing ingredients together with a generous seasoning of salt and pepper in a small pitcher or bowl.

Holding the stalk end, make an incision down one side of each eggplant without cutting all the way through and open out the eggplant to reveal the flesh inside. Gently shake off any excess liquid or pat it off with paper towels. Divide the dressing between the eggplants and very gently mash it into the flesh a little with a fork. Sprinkle over the scallions, cilantro, and pul biber, top with the chopped peanuts, and serve.

Serve with Aegean Giant Couscous Salad (see page 10) or Pan-fried Salmon with Barberry Butter (see page 133).

Burnt Zucchini with Lemon & Feta Yogurt

Zucchini really do get a bad rap sometimes, but they are a firm favorite of mine. My preferred method to cook them is always to roast them in the oven. Here, the charring really gives them an added depth and dimension that works wonderfully with yogurt and feta, and the spike of lemon and mint freshens this beauty of a recipe so well. Perfect for dipping toasted bread into or eating on the side of roasted meats, such as lamb and chicken.

SERVES 4 TO 6

4 zucchini, halved lengthwise and
  cut into 1¼-inch chunks

olive oil

2 cups thick Greek yogurt

7oz feta cheese, broken into
  small chunks

3 scallions, thinly sliced

1 fat garlic clove, minced

finely grated zest of 1 unwaxed lemon

1 small pack (about 1oz) of mint,
  leaves picked, rolled up tightly and
  thinly sliced into ribbons, reserving
  some for garnish

2 teaspoons dried wild oregano,
  reserving some for garnish

Maldon sea salt flakes and freshly
  ground black pepper

toasted pitta breads, to serve

Preheat your oven to its highest setting. Line a large baking pan with parchment paper.

Spread the zucchini chunks out on the lined pan, drizzle with olive oil, and roast for 18 to 20 minutes until deeply charred in parts. Remove from the oven and let cool.

Put all the remaining ingredients into a mixing bowl. Add a drizzle of olive oil, season well with salt and pepper, and mix everything together.

Once the zucchini have cooled, chop them coarsely, then add them to the yogurt mixture and stir together. Drizzle with olive oil, scatter with more mint and oregano, and serve with toasted pitta breads.

Serve with Root Vegetable, Chickpea, Feta & Barberry Pie (see page 149) or Cabbage "Bowl" Dolma (see page 147).

Cabbage "Bowl" Dolma

When I was a kid, onion and cabbage dolmas were always my favorite because they would absorb the poaching liquid and sweeten it in a way that vine leaves didn't quite do. Even though "bowl" dolma (using a small bowl to help form the dolma) is not a classic recipe, anything that makes my life easier is welcome in my repertoire. While Persians like meat in their classic dolma, I've made these vegan to suit everyone as either a main or a side to meat or fish. Note that dolmas ALWAYS taste better made a day ahead.

SERVES 4 TO 6

1 large head of Savoy cabbage, leaves separated

olive oil

1 large onion, finely chopped

⅓ cup tomato paste

2 teaspoons garlic granules

1 teaspoon paprika

1 teaspoon ground cumin

1 teaspoon pul biber chile flakes

½ teaspoon ground cinnamon

1¼ cups basmati rice

1 small pack (about 1oz) of flat-leaf parsley, finely chopped

1 small pack (about 1oz) of chives, thinly sliced

1 small pack (about 1oz) of fresh cilantro, finely chopped

1 small pack (about 1oz) of dill, finely chopped

Maldon sea salt flakes and freshly ground black pepper

For the tomato sauce

14oz can diced tomatoes

2 teaspoons superfine sugar

good squeeze of lemon juice

For the poaching liquid

2½ cups boiling water

2 vegetable or vegan stock cubes

2 tablespoons tomato paste

2 tablespoons superfine sugar

To make the tomato sauce, place a small saucepan over low-medium heat, add the ingredients, along with a generous amount of salt and pepper, and bring to a gentle boil. Cook for 20 minutes, stirring regularly, until reduced to a thick saucelike consistency. Remove from the heat and let cool. Using a hand-held stick blender, blitz the sauce until smooth.

continued overleaf

Bring a large saucepan of water to a boil, add the cabbage leaves, and let boil for about 10 minutes or so until tender and flexible. Drain and cover with cold water to cool them down.

Preheat the oven to 400°F. Select a medium-large ovenproof dish.

Place a skillet over medium-high heat, drizzle in some olive oil, and fry the onion until softened but not colored. Add the tomato paste, garlic granules, spices, and a generous seasoning of salt and pepper. Cook the spice mixture for 2 to 3 minutes, stirring regularly. Add the rice and quickly stir to coat in the mixture, then add the herbs, mix well again, and remove from the heat but continue to mix until everything is evenly combined. Set aside.

Drain the cabbage leaves and pat them dry. Choose the largest leaves and cut out and discard the cores. Line the bottom of a very small bowl, about 4 inches or so in diameter, with a cabbage leaf. Divide the rice mixture into 8 to 10 portions, depending on how many large leaves you get from the cabbage (you can also overlay smaller and broken leaves), then place a portion on the leaf in the bowl and wrap the leaf around the filling to enclose it. Carefully remove the dolma from the bowl. Repeat with the remaining cabbage leaves and the rice mixture.

Select a deep ovenproof dish or baking pan that all the dolma will fit snugly into. Drizzle olive oil in the bottom of the dish and line it with any remaining leaves. Carefully transfer all the dolma into the dish.

Stir the poaching liquid ingredients together until the stock cubes have dissolved, then pour into the dish (the liquid level should be high enough to cook the rice). Pour the tomato sauce over the dolma, then cover the dish with a double layer of alumium foil and bake in the lowest part of the oven for an hour. Lower the oven temperature to 350°F then bake for a further 30 minutes. Remove from the oven and let cool. These are best made the day before eating to allow the flavors to intensify, so refrigerate them until you are ready to serve the next day.

To reheat, preheat the oven to 400°F and remove the dolma from the fridge. Lift the foil covering from the dolma and add a splash of water, then replace the foil. Place in the hot oven for 20 to 25 minutes, or until warmed through. These are best eaten warm rather than piping hot.

Serve with Butterflied Lamb with Tahini Garlic Yogurt (see page 123) or Burnt Zucchini with Lemon & Feta Yogurt (see page 145).

Root Vegetable, Chickpea, Feta & Barberry Pie

I first created this recipe for a cookery class in the run-up to Christmas when I wanted to give students a wonderful vegetarian dish that would be perfect as a main course for the festive table. Fast forward many years later and it's simply a wonderful dish to serve at any time. However, its use of root vegetables lends it particularly well to the fall and winter months. This dish is incredibly forgiving because, no matter how you make it, it will look beautiful and therefore makes a worthy centerpiece whatever the season. What's more, it's substantial and delicious.

SERVES 4 TO 6

about 2 tablespoons vegetable oil

1 large onion, finely chopped

2 fat garlic cloves, minced

pinch of saffron threads, finely crumbled or ground using a mortar and pestle

2 parsnips, peeled and coarsely grated

10½oz celery root, peeled and coarsely grated

14oz can chickpeas, drained

1 teaspoon sumac

1 heaped teaspoon ground coriander

1 teaspoon ground cinnamon

1 teaspoon pul biber chile flakes

2 large carrots, peeled and coarsely grated

finely grated zest of 1 unwaxed lemon and juice of ½

1 heaped tablespoon honey, plus extra for drizzling

1 small pack (about 1oz) of dill, finely chopped

1 small pack (about 1oz) of flat-leaf parsley, finely chopped

2 good handfuls of dried barberries

1⅓ cups finely crumbled feta cheese

¾ cup pistachio nuts, coarsely chopped

6 sheets of filo pastry (each about 19 x 10 inches)

⅔ stick butter, melted

Maldon sea salt flakes and freshly ground black pepper

Preheat the oven to 425°F. Select a 10-inch round ovenproof dish.

Place a large skillet over medium heat, add the vegetable oil, and fry the onion until soft but not colored too much. Add the garlic and cook, stirring well, for a couple of minutes.

continued overleaf

Stir the saffron through the onion mixture and then add the parsnips and celery root first, stirring for a couple of minutes, before mixing in the chickpeas and spices. Then add the carrots and a generous amount of salt and pepper. Remove the pan from the heat, add the lemon zest and juice, honey, herbs, and barberries. Stir until combined, then carefully fold in the feta and pistachios.

Lay 3 filo pastry sheets in the bottom of the ovenproof dish at different angles and with enough hanging over the edges of the dish to cover the top of the pie, but ensuring the bottom is completely covered. Brush generously with melted butter and then tip in the root vegetable mixture and compress to fill the dish. Crumple up the edges of the loose pastry around the sides of the pie to make a ruffled edge, like a kind of crust. Brush the exposed edges with butter. Crumple up the remaining filo pastry sheets loosely on top to cover the surface and then brush with the remaining butter. Bake for 25 to 30 minutes until nicely golden brown.

Remove from the oven, let cool for a few minutes, and then serve with a generous drizzle of honey on top if desired.

Serve with Mama Ghanoush (see page 158).

Cabbage with Tamarind, Maple & Black Pepper Butter

It's fair to say that I eat a lot of cabbage of every description. I use it in different ways, from raw to cooked, from dolmas to pastas and stir-fries. Nothing is exempt from improvement with a little added cabbage! This recipe contains a method I absolutely love to use when cooking cabbage. The butter really takes the cabbage to another level and makes this humble brassica something altogether very special and unique.

SERVES 2 TO 4

olive oil

1 large head of hispi cabbage, stalk left on, quartered

½ cup cold water

½ stick butter

1 heaped tablespoon tamarind paste

2 tablespoons maple syrup

1 teaspoon coarse freshly ground black pepper

Maldon sea salt flakes

Place a large skillet over medium heat and drizzle in some olive oil. Arrange the cabbage wedges in the pan, sitting on one cut side and with the stalk ends in the center of the pan, and fry for 5 minutes. Pour in the cold water, increase the heat a little, and cover the pan with a lid. Let it cook for about 6 to 7 minutes until the water has evaporated.

Remove the lid and turn the cabbage wedges over to cook on the other cut side for 3 to 4 minutes, uncovered, then add the butter. Mix the tamarind, maple syrup, and pepper together, then add to the pan with a good seasoning of salt and stir it into the melted butter quickly. A little charring is good, but take care to prevent it from burning. Baste the cabbage as best you can, then flip the quarters back onto the other side and keep basting for a few more minutes. Serve drizzled with any remaining flavored butter from the pan.

Serve with Pan-fried Salmon with Barberry Butter (see page 133).

Charred Broccoli with Lemons, Chiles & Yogurt

Broccoli is one green vegetable that everyone in our house likes, and since I've become a step-parent, I've realized this may be as good as it gets . So, I am constantly making things with broccoli to ensure some vegetables other than potatoes are being consumed. Truth is, I absolutely love the stuff myself, whether the classic large florets or broccolini, and I do like to add it to many dishes for flavor and texture. While I enjoy it simply with salt and pepper, sometimes a change is needed and a few big flavor items are required to give things a little lift. Sour, spicy, tangy, and delicious, this dish is a fantastic way to keep broccoli on the menu.

SERVES 3 TO 4

1 large head or 2 small heads
   of broccoli

olive oil

½ cup Greek yogurt or plant-based-
   yogurt, thinned down with water
   to the pouring consistency
   of heavy cream

3 pickled red chiles, thinly sliced

1 to 2 preserved lemons (or to taste),
   seeded and finely chopped

1 teaspoon nigella seeds

Maldon sea salt flakes and freshly
   ground black pepper

Break the broccoli into florets, then peel the large central stalk with a vegetable peeler and slice into disks. Put all the florets and stalk pieces into a large heatproof bowl. Add enough boiling water to cover, ensuring they are all submerged. Let blanch in the hot water for 5 minutes, then transfer to a colander and let stand.

Heat a ridged grill pan over high heat, and once hot, return the broccoli to the bowl, drizzle generously with olive oil, and turn to coat. Add the broccoli to the pan and let cook for a few minutes on both sides until it bears char marks. Remove from the pan and place on a platter, then season well with pepper and just a little salt. Drizzle with the loosened yogurt, sprinkle with the pickled chiles, preserved lemons, and nigella seeds, and then serve.

Serve with Baked Vegetable & Feta Layers (see page 138) or Ras el Hanout, Orange & Lamb Rib Chop Platter (see page 109).

Bhaji Buns

I love an onion bhaji and this is my homage to them, using kitchen-cupboard spices. I have paired this with a soft white dinner roll, taking inspiration from chaat street food where treats are laden with yogurt, tamarind sauce, herbs, and sev (a crispy fine noodle). But to make it easier for you, I've used cornflakes to add crunch.

MAKES 4

2 large onions, finely chopped

⅓ cup gram (chickpea) flour

1 teaspoon baking powder

2 teaspoons ground turmeric

1 teaspoon pul biber chile flakes

1 teaspoon cumin seeds

1 teaspoon garlic granules

juice of ½ lemon

½ small pack (about ½oz) of fresh cilantro, finely chopped, plus extra leaves for garnish

vegetable oil, for frying

Maldon sea salt flakes and freshly ground black pepper

To serve

4 soft white dinner rolls

sweet tamarind sauce or mango chutney

Greek yogurt or plant-based yogurt

pomegranate seeds

handful of unsweetened cornflakes or plain potato chips

Put the onions into a mixing bowl with a generous amount of salt (this will any encourage moisture to be released, which helps bind the mixture) and stir very well with a fork. Let stand for 10 minutes.

Stir the onions again, add all the remaining ingredients, except the oil, with a good seasoning of black pepper. Mix everything together until you have a cohesive batter. Let the batter stand for 10 minutes.

Meanwhile, heat a large skillet over medium-high heat, pour in about 1 inch of vegetable oil, and bring to frying temperature. (Add a pinch of the batter. If it sizzles immediately, the oil is hot enough.) Line a large plate with a double layer of paper towels.

Stir the onion mixture once more, then use your hands to form 4 round patties (the mixture will be wet, but don't worry, just shape them as best you can), then flatten them. Fry the patties 1 or 2 at a time, depending on how many you can fit in your skillet, for about 4 to 5 minutes or so until deep brown on the underside. Then flip them over gently using a slotted spoon and fork until deep brown all over. Remove with the slotted spoon and transfer to the paper-lined plate to drain. Serve in soft white dinner rolls, and top with tamarind sauce or mango chutney, yogurt, pomegranate seeds, cilantro leaves, and cornflakes or plain potato chips. This needs no accompaniment.

Mama Ghanoush

It would be fair to say that Mama Ghanoush is not actually an authentic Middle Eastern recipe, so I would like you to think of her as baba's spicy other half. With all the joys of a classic baba ghanoush, and a few additions including pul biber, yogurt, and fresh herbs to give it a little lift, try this when you feel like having something with a more complex and punchy flavor.

SERVES 4 TO 6

4 large eggplants

2 fat garlic cloves, crushed or minced

½ small packet (about ½oz) of fresh cilantro, finely chopped, some reserved for garnish

½ small packet (about ½oz) of flat-leaf parsley, finely chopped, some reserved for garnish

1 heaped teaspoon pul biber chile flakes, plus extra for garnish

⅔ cup Greek yogurt or plant-based yogurt

⅓ cup tahini

finely grated zest and juice of 1 fat unwaxed lemon

olive oil

Maldon sea salt flakes and freshly ground black pepper

toasted mini pitta breads, to serve

Smoke the eggplants whole over an open flame either on a barbecue or over a gas stove, using long-handled tongs to continually turn them, until the skin has crackled and become ashen all over, the eggplants have collapsed by half, and the flesh is completely soft on the inside. Remove from the heat and let the eggplants cool until you can handle them.

Holding the stalk end, make an incision down one side of each eggplant without cutting all the way through and open out the eggplants to reveal the flesh inside. Scoop out the flesh into a sieve to strain off any excess liquid, and discard the skins.

Put the eggplant flesh and all the remaining ingredients into a mixing bowl with a good drizzle of olive oil and a generous seasoning of salt and pepper and mix well. Taste and adjust the seasoning if desired.

To serve, spread thinly over a large plate, drizzle with more olive oil, and scatter with the reserved herbs and pul biber. Serve with toasted mini pitta breads.

Serve with Nargessi Kofta Loaf (see page 107), or Butterflied Lamb with Tahini Garlic Yogurt (see page 123), or Afghani Polow (see page 191).

Nimroo Mirzai

This is my own creation based on the popular Persian dish, *mirza ghasemi* (which you can find the recipe for in my book *Persiana*), using smoked eggplants, tomatoes, and eggs, and finished with walnuts. It has all the joys of the former but in a breakfast dish that scrambles eggs the way Persians do to make a classic *nimroo tomat* (scrambled eggs and tomatoes). The addition of garlic, cooked in a sweet, mellow way along with the tomato and turmeric, feels like it shouldn't work , but it does! Perfect on thick white or sourdough toast, it's incredibly good at any time of day.

SERVES 4

olive oil

4 garlic cloves, minced

1 teaspoon ground turmeric

2 tablespoons tomato paste

2 large tomatoes, cut into 8

4 eggs

1 to 3 tablespoons of butter

Maldon sea salt flakes and freshly
    ground black pepper

toasted bread or flatbread, to serve

Place a skillet over medium heat and drizzle in a little olive oil, then add the garlic and stir for a minute or so until it begins to cook without coloring.

Add the turmeric, tomato paste, and a generous amount of pepper and some salt. Mix it all together and cook, stirring, for a couple of minutes. Add the fresh tomatoes and stir again (this should all be sizzling but not burning). Then cover the pan with a lid and cook for 6 to 7 minutes until the tomatoes are cooked through, stirring occasionally to ensure the mixture doesn't burn.

Stir well and then increase the heat just a little. Crack the eggs into the pan, add the butter, and begin scrambling the eggs into the mixture. The texture should be wet and loose so don't expect it to look like scrambled eggs. Keep stirring until the eggs are cooked, then serve with toasted bread or flatbread. This needs no accompaniment.

Marinated Halloumi Skewers

Whether you call it halloumi or hellim, it is the one ingredient that I always have in my refrigerator for when you need rescuing and you have nothing else. These skewers are Mediterranean in essence, but with a little spice to boot. My favorite way to eat them is to place the skewer onto some flatbread and slide the ingredients off, then drizzle with a little honey (trust me on this), add a squeeze of lemon juice, and a little chilli sauce. Roll it up and tuck in. If you don't have skewers, simply roast the ingredients on a baking pan.

MAKES 3

9oz block of halloumi cheese, cut into 6 cubes

½ red bell pepper, cored, seeded, and cut into 6 pieces

½ yellow bell pepper, cored, seeded, and cut into 6 pieces

6 cherry tomatoes, halved

1 teaspoon dried mint

1 teaspoon dried wild oregano

1 teaspoon ground coriander

1 teaspoon paprika

3 tablespoons garlic oil

freshly ground black pepper

To serve

3 flatbreads

chilli sauce of your choice

lemon wedges

honey, for drizzling (optional)

Preheat your oven to its highest setting. Line a baking pan with parchment paper.

Put the halloumi, bell peppers, and tomatoes into a mixing bowl, add the dried herbs, spices, garlic oil, and a generous amount of black pepper and gently mix together to evenly coat the ingredients in the oil and seasonings.

Divide the ingredients into 3 equal portions and push each portion onto a wooden or metal skewer. Place the skewers onto the lined pan and roast for 15 to 16 minutes until cooked. You can also cook them on a barbecue, turning frequently (if using wooden skewers, presoak them in cold water for about 30 minutes). Serve with flatbreads, your favorite chilli sauce, lemon wedges for squeezing over, and a drizzle of honey if desired.

Serve with Cauliflower & Lentil Salad (see page 17) or Warm Orzo, Black-eyed Pea & Herb Salad (see page 42).

Ras el Hanout & Sweet Potatoes with Tahini Yogurt & Herb Oil

Sweet potatoes are wonderfully versatile and their natural sweetness makes them a perfect match for spices and other aromatic flavors. You can rely on the ras el hanout spice blend to do most of the work here. Just roast the sweet potatoes, add a simple tahini yogurt, and serve with a quick herb oil, pine nuts, and pomegranate seeds.

SERVES 4 TO 6

4 sweet potatoes, peeled and cut into
   disks ½ inch in thickness

¼ cup olive oil

2 heaped tablespoons ras el hanout

2 tablespoons pine nuts

good handful of pomegranate seeds

Maldon sea salt flakes and freshly
   ground black pepper

For the herb oil

½ small packet (about ½oz) of flat-leaf
   parsley

½ small packet (about ½oz) of dill

½ small packet (about ½oz) of fresh
   cilantro

juice of ½ lemon

about 3 to 4 tablespoons olive oil,
   or as needed

For the tahini yogurt

⅓ cup Greek yogurt (not the thick kind)
   or plant-based yogurt

¼ cup tahini

Preheat the oven to 425°F. Line a large baking pan with parchment paper.

Place the sweet potato slices on the lined pan. Drizzle the slices with the olive oil, sprinkle with the ras el hanout, and add a generous amount of salt. Then use your hands to rub the mixture evenly all over them. Arrange the slices in a single layer and roast for 30 minutes or until cooked through.

Meanwhile, for the herb oil, put the herbs, lemon juice, olive oil (enough to enable the mixture to spin), and some salt and pepper into a blender and blitz until smooth.

Mix the yogurt and tahini together in a small bowl and season well with salt and pepper.

Remove the sweet potatoes from the oven and transfer to a platter. Drizzle with the tahini yogurt followed by the herb oil. Scatter with the pine nuts and pomegranate seeds and serve.

Serve with Spicy Keema Rolls (see page 73) or Pan-fried Salmon with Barberry Butter (see page 133).

Spice-Roasted Potatoes with Bell Pepper, Tomato & Harissa Sauce

This is a lovely dish that makes the potato feel less of a sideshow and more of a star. Think of it as comfort food with a Middle Eastern twist, which can very well stand alone but, for the creative among you, can easily be paired with fried eggs, halloumi, or even simply some crumbled feta on top.

SERVES 6

2¼lb potatoes, peeled and cut into
    1-inch cubes
2 teaspoons paprika
2 teaspoons ground turmeric
2 teaspoons cumin seeds
3 tablespoons garlic oil or olive oil
Maldon sea salt flakes and freshly
    ground black pepper
handful of chopped mint, parsley,
    fresh cilantro, or dill, to garnish
crumbled feta, to serve (optional)

For the sauce
olive oil
2 garlic cloves, bashed and thinly
    sliced
9oz (drained weight) roasted
    red bell peppers from a jar,
    coarsely chopped
14oz can diced tomatoes
1 heaped tablespoon rose harissa
1 tablespoon superfine sugar

Preheat the oven to 425°F. Line a baking pan with parchment paper. Place the potato pieces on the lined pan. Mix the spices and garlic oil or olive oil together and drizzle it over the pieces, then use your hands to coat them evenly in the spiced oil. Spread out in a single layer, season well with salt and pepper, and roast for 30 minutes or until tender and cooked through.

Meanwhile, to make the sauce, drizzle some olive oil into a saucepan, add the garlic slices, and cook over medium heat for 2 minutes. Add the bell peppers, tomatoes, and rose harissa along with a generous amount of salt and cook, stirring, for a further 2 minutes. Add the sugar, stir well, and cook over medium-high heat for 20 minutes, stirring regularly to ensure it doesn't burn. Remove from the heat and, using a hand-held stick blender, blitz the sauce until smooth. Taste and adjust the seasoning if desired.

Arrange the potatoes on a plate, pour the sauce over them, then scatter with the herbs and feta (if using).

Serve with Herb Koftas with Warm Yogurt Sauce & Spiced Mint Butter (see page 92) or Butterflied Lamb with Tahini Garlic Yogurt (see page 123).

Fried Potatoes, Spinach & Eggs with Yogurt & Spiced Butter

This is a recipe suitable for breakfast, lunch, or dinner. The fried potatoes can carry a multitude of flavors and spices, and this combination is wonderfully simple yet indulgent courtesy of the spice butter finish.

SERVES 2 TO 4

olive oil

1lb 2oz potatoes, peeled and cut into ½-inch cubes

2 teaspoons dried fenugreek leaves

4½oz baby spinach

5 scallions, thinly sliced

4 eggs

½ cup Greek yogurt

Maldon sea salt flakes and freshly ground black pepper

For the spiced butter

½ teaspoon coriander seeds

½ teaspoon cumin seeds

1 teaspoon pul biber chile flakes

2 tablespoons butter

flatbreads, to serve

For the spiced butter, heat a small dry saucepan over medium-high heat, add the coriander and cumin seeds, and toast for 1 to 2 minutes until they release their aroma, shaking the pan intermittently to prevent them from burning. Remove from the heat and lightly crush using a mortar and pestle until coarsely ground (not ground down to a powder). Tip the ground seeds back into the pan along with the pul biber, and set aside.

Place a skillet over medium-high heat, pour in some olive oil, and fry the potatoes until they begin to brown all over, stirring occasionally. Cover the pan with a lid and cook for a further 10 minutes, shaking the pan regularly to prevent the potatoes from sticking, until tender. Remove the lid, add the fenugreek, and mix it in to coat the potatoes. Push the potatoes to one side of the pan, add the spinach, and cook for 2 to 3 minutes until wilted, then mix into the potatoes. Add the scallions and season everything well with salt and pepper. Make 4 wells in the potato mixture and crack an egg into each one, then reduce to low-medium heat, replace the lid, and cook for 5 to 6 minutes.

Melt the butter in the pan with the spices and season with salt and pepper. Once the eggs are cooked, dollop with the yogurt, then drizzle with the spiced butter, and serve with flatbreads and a grinding of black pepper. This needs no accompaniment.

Spiced Tahini & Honey-Roasted Eggplants

Since adopting this technique, I have glazed eggplants with every conceivable kind of sauce you could imagine. This method is so incredibly good for cooking eggplants that it should give you the confidence to experiment with other flavors, and I would encourage you to do just that. But while you're here, this is a fantastic combination of ingredients that gives a rich, nutty, and chewy surface when slightly cooled. I ask you, what's not to love about that?

MAKES 4

2 large eggplants

¼ cup garlic oil

3 tablespoons tahini

2 tablespoons honey
 (if vegan, use maple syrup)

1 teaspoon garlic granules

1 teaspoon pul biber chile flakes

Maldon sea salt flakes and freshly
 ground black pepper

Preheat the oven to 400°F. Line a baking pan with parchment paper.

Using a sharp knife, cut the eggplants in half lengthwise, then score a criss-cross pattern in the cut sides and place, cut-side up, on the lined pan. Brush the scored flesh of each half with the garlic oil and roast for 30 minutes or until cooked through.

Meanwhile, mix together the tahini, honey (or maple syrup), garlic granules, pul biber, and a generous amount of salt and pepper in a small bowl until smooth.

Remove the eggplants from the oven, divide the tahini mixture between the halves, and spread it all over each surface. Roast for a further 10 to 12 minutes until lovely and golden brown on the surface. Remove from the oven and serve.

Serve with Arugula Salad with Halloumi, Blood Oranges & Pistachio Nuts (see page 18) or Nargessi Kofta Loaf (see page 107).

Roasted Eggplants with Spicy Peanut Sauce

When I consider the eggplant, I often wonder how many more eggplant recipes I have left in me. Then I think of another flavor combination that I think may work well (usually inspired by what's in my store cupboard) and the rest, as they say, is history. Eggplants are endlessly versatile and this dish, inspired by satay sauce flavors—plus the heat of harissa—works so well. Please trust me and make it for yourself!

SERVES 4

2 large eggplants, quartered lengthwise

olive oil

For the sauce

2 tablespoons smooth peanut butter

2 tablespoons honey (if vegan, use maple syrup)

1 tablespoon rose harissa

1 tablespoon rice vinegar

1 tablespoon lukewarm water

Maldon sea salt flakes

To serve

generous handful of salted peanuts, coarsely chopped

2 scallions, thinly sliced from root to tip

good handful of chopped fresh cilantro leaves

Preheat the oven to 400°F. Line a baking pan with parchment paper.

Place the eggplants on the lined pan, rub the exposed flesh with olive oil, and roast for 30 minutes until soft and cooked through.

Meanwhile, for the sauce, put the peanut butter, honey (or maple syrup), harissa, vinegar, and a good pinch of salt into a small bowl and mix together. Then add the water to thin the mixture down and stir to combine.

Once cooked, arrange the roasted eggplants on a platter. Drizzle with the sauce, scatter with the peanuts, scallions, and cilantro, and serve.

Serve with Spicy Keema Rolls (see page 73) or Sweet Potato & Chickpea Balls (see page 86).

Oven-Baked Spicy Chickpeas & Eggplants with Yogurt & Herbs

The convenience of cooking everything together in the oven on one pan appeals to me greatly and means I can disappear for a while and get on with other things. This dish can even be served straight from the oven to the table. Why bother with the extra dishwashing when it will only get devoured in minutes anyway?

SERVES 4 TO 6

1 teaspoon paprika

1 teaspoon ground turmeric

1 teaspoon ground cumin

1 teaspoon ground coriander

olive oil

14oz can chickpeas, drained

2 large eggplants, peeled, halved
    widthwise, and cut into wedges
    1 inch in thickness

Maldon sea salt flakes and freshly
    ground black pepper

To serve

⅔ cup Greek or plant-based yogurt

generous handful of chopped mixed
    herb leaves (I used a mixture of
    fresh cilantro, dill, and mint)

3 tablespoons tahini, thinned down
    with lukewarm water

3 tablespoons pomegranate molasses

generous handful of storebought
    crispy fried onions

Preheat the oven to 400°F. Line your largest baking pan with parchment paper.

Put all the spices, 3 tablespoons olive oil, and a generous amount of salt and pepper into a mixing bowl and stir to combine. Add the chickpeas and stir until evenly coated.

Arrange the eggplant wedges in a single layer on the lined pan, drizzle generously with olive oil, rub it in all over the wedges, then season well with salt and pepper. Make some space to add the chickpeas to the pan in a single layer (try to avoid covering the eggplant wedges). Roast for 30 to 35 minutes until nicely browned all over. Remove from the oven, and transfer to a platter if you prefer.

Ensure the yogurt is a pouring consistency, adding a little lukewarm water to thin it down if necessary, then drizzle it all over the roasted eggplant wedges and chickpeas. Scatter with the herbs and drizzle with the loosened tahini. Top everything with the pomegranate molasses and then the crispy onions and serve.

Serve with Spicy Keema Rolls (see page 73) or Dried Lime & Spice-marinated Lamb Chops (see page 95).

Roasted Tomatoes with Labneh & Sumac Spice Oil

One of the most classic Persian accompaniments is the whole flame-roasted tomato. A staple served with every kebab, it's simply made by placing a whole tomato on a charcoal grill and roasting until the skin is somewhat charred in parts and the soft flesh inside is bursting with juices. This dish is inspired by my love for the roasted tomato, but reimagined for indoor cooking. Served with labneh (which Persians serve with everything) and a little spice oil for adding depth and flavor, it really is a wonderful dish and perfect alongside roasted or barbecued meats and vegetables.

SERVES 4 TO 6

2 very large and 4 to 6 medium
    tomatoes, halved
olive oil
2 cups labneh or thick Greek yogurt
    or plant-based yogurt
Maldon sea salt flakes and freshly
    ground black pepper

For the spice oil
¼ to ⅓ cup olive oil
3 garlic cloves, thinly sliced
1 teaspoon fennel seeds
1 teaspoon cumin seeds
1 teaspoon sumac
1 teaspoon pul biber chile flakes

Preheat your oven to its highest setting. Line a large baking pan with parchment paper.

Place the tomato halves, cut-side up, on the lined pan and drizzle with olive oil. Roast for 20 to 25 minutes or until nicely charred, then remove from the oven and set aside.

For the spice oil, place a small saucepan over low-medium heat, add the olive oil, garlic slices, and the fennel and cumin seeds. Cook gently for 8 to 10 minutes until the garlic is cooked but not browned too much. Remove from the heat, add the sumac and pul biber, season with salt and pepper, and stir to combine.

Spread the labneh or yogurt out on a large platter until it reaches the edges, then arrange the roasted tomatoes over the labneh or yogurt and season with salt and pepper. Drizzle with the spice oil and serve.

Serve with Afghani Polow (see page 191) or Dampokhtak (see page 196).

Turmeric-Spiced Yogurt with White Beans

This is one of those recipes that shouldn't work, but it does. Spiced beans are fried in a skillet, enrobed in yogurt, and cooked until the yogurt is hot. If the yogurt curdles slightly, this is nothing to worry about. Everything will still taste just as nice. Really easy, really delicious, and unlike anything I've tasted before, it's perfect on toast or with flatbreads.

SERVES 4 TO 6

2 tablespoons olive oil

2 teaspoons cumin seeds

2 teaspoons coriander seeds

2 x 14oz cans cannellini beans, drained
    and rinsed

2 garlic cloves, minced

2 teaspoons ground turmeric

½ teaspoon dried red chile flakes

1 cup Greek yogurt or plant-based yogurt

Maldon sea salt flakes and freshly ground
    black pepper

Heat a large skillet over medium-high heat, add the olive oil, then the cumin and coriander seeds, and fry for a couple of minutes.

Add the beans and garlic and stir to coat them in the spice oil. Add the turmeric, chile flakes, and a generous amount of salt and pepper. Stir again and let it cook for a few minutes.

Stir in the yogurt and keep gently stirring it through the beans while you cook for a few more minutes until the yogurt sauce has reduced and just about coats the beans. Serve seasoned with extra black pepper.

Serve with Nargessi Kofta Loaf (see page 107) or Marinated Halloumi Skewers (see page 162).

Tomato & Feta Fritters

This has a very Greek vibe to it. I love tomatoes and feta together, so combining them in these fritters was a no-brainer. The punch of tarragon is also really lovely with the tomato combo, and I hope you like these as much as I do. I love to serve them with a sort of tzatziki sauce without the cucumber, as below.

MAKES 10 TO 12

1lb 2oz large plum tomatoes, seeded

1 teaspoon dried wild oregano

¼ cup finely chopped tarragon leaves

⅔ cup crumbled feta cheese

5 scallions, thinly sliced

⅓ cup all-purpose flour

1 teaspoon baking powder

vegetable oil, for frying

Maldon sea salt flakes and freshly
   ground black pepper

For the sauce

⅔ cup Greek yogurt

1 small garlic clove, crushed

1 teaspoon dried wild oregano

Pat dry the tomato flesh with paper towels, then coarsely chop into small cubes. Place the cubes into a mixing bowl, leaving any remaining liquid behind. Add the oregano, tarragon, and some salt and pepper and stir together really well. Let stand for 5 minutes, then stir again before adding the feta and scallions and stirring to combine. Add the flour and baking powder and mix together with a spoon until you have a batter, then set aside.

Meanwhile, mix the sauce ingredients together in a small bowl and season with salt and pepper.

Heat a large skillet over medium-high heat, pour in about 1 inch of vegetable oil and bring to frying temperature. (Add a little bit of the batter. If it sizzles immediately, the oil is hot enough.) Line a large plate with a double layer of paper towels.

Mix the batter again with the spoon and test to see if you can scoop up a tablespoonful and lightly pat it into a ball (you may need a little more flour to bind the mixture, so add sparingly). Form the batter into 10 to 12 balls, add to the hot oil in batches, and fry gently for a couple of minutes or so on each side until crisp and browned. Remove with a slotted spoon and transfer to the paper-lined plate to drain. Serve with the sauce alongside.

Serve with Herb Koftas with Warm Yogurt Sauce & Spiced Mint Butter (see page 92) or Mama Ghanoush (see page 158).

Sweet & Spicy Crunchy Eggplants

When I first made this recipe, I wanted to shout it from the rooftops because it was so insanely delicious that I felt it needed to be shared. The wonderful flavor of the Thai holy basil really takes it to the next level, and the crunchy coating gives the eggplant an extra dimension. I can eat a whole pan of this with just some steamed rice on the side. No other accompaniment is needed to keep me happy.

SERVES 4

vegetable oil, for frying

2 large eggplants, peeled, halved widthwise, and cut into batons ¾ inch in thickness

⅓ cup plus 1 tablespoon cornstarch

6 fat garlic cloves, thinly sliced

2 heaped tablespoons rose harissa

3 tablespoons superfine sugar

juice of 1 fat lime

3 tablespoons light soy sauce

1 cup cold water

leaves from 1 small pack (about 1oz) of fresh Thai holy basil (or use ordinary basil or fresh cilantro)

Maldon sea salt flakes and freshly ground black pepper

Heat a large, deep skillet over medium-high heat, pour in 1 inch of vegetable oil, and bring to frying temperature. (Add a breadcrumb. If it sizzles, the oil is hot enough.) Line a plate with a double layer of paper towels.

Put the eggplants, the ⅓ cup of cornstarch, and a very generous seasoning of salt and pepper into a mixing bowl and stir together, ensuring the cornstarch coats the eggplants all over, leaving no cornstarch behind.

Add the eggplant batons to the hot oil and fry a few at a time in 2 to 3 batches for a good few minutes until they are nicely browned on all sides. You don't want to brown the outside too quickly otherwise the eggplant flesh inside won't be cooked. If necessary, let the oil cool down a little before frying the next batch. Remove the cooked batches with a slotted spoon and transfer to the paper-lined plate to drain.

Heat a saucepan over medium heat, drizzle in 2 tablespoons of oil, and fry the garlic slices until translucent and lightly sizzling. Add the harissa, sugar, lime juice, soy sauce, and remaining tablespoon of cornstarch and mix together well. Gradually pour in the water, stirring well until evenly combined, and cook until the sauce looks glossy and has reduced in consistency. Stir in the Thai basil leaves, then add the crunchy eggplants, working carefully and quickly to coat them in the sauce. Serve immediately.

Serve with Charred Broccoli with Lemons, Chiles & Yogurt (see page 154) or Marinated Halloumi Skewers (see page 162).

Tangy Pomegranate with Tomato & Eggplants

This recipe feels familiar in a chutney sort of way, almost like a fresh eggplant chutney that's more of a side dish than merely a relish or sauce. Some earthy spicing and sweetness rounded off with the sharp tang of pomegranate molasses make this a perfect dish to cut through the richness of roasted meats and kebabs. It's also great with toasted pitta breads or sourdough.

SERVES 4

olive oil

1 large onion, finely chopped

4 fat garlic cloves, thinly sliced

1 teaspoon fennel seeds

1 teaspoon cumin seeds

1 teaspoon ground turmeric

3 large eggplants, smoked (see page 142 for method), peeled, and flesh drained of excess liquid

2 tablespoons tomato paste

⅓ cup pomegranate molasses

2 tablespoons vegan red wine vinegar

2 tablespoons superfine sugar

Maldon sea salt flakes and freshly ground black pepper

toasted pitta, to serve

Heat a skillet over medium heat, add a good drizzle of olive oil, and cook the onion and garlic until softened. Stir in the fennel and cumin seeds followed by the turmeric and stir well. Add the cooked eggplant flesh and a generous amount of salt and pepper and mix really well. Then add the tomato paste, pomegranate molasses, vinegar, and sugar and again stir really well until all is evenly combined. Cook, stirring regularly, for 10 to 15 minutes.

Reduce the heat slightly and let cook for a further 20 minutes or so, stirring occasionally. Taste and adjust the seasoning if desired. Serve warm with toasted pitta breads.

Serve with Afghani Polow (see page 191) or Ground Lamb Börek (see page 103).

Pasta, Noodles & Grains

Baghala Polow with Saffron-Flecked Lamb Shanks

This recipe holds so many memories for me, as my grandmother's sister, Khaleh ("Aunty") Gohar Malek, was the only really good cook in our family, and whenever she made this it was pure joy in every mouthful. The smell, the glistening buttery rice, and those juicy, soft lamb shanks flecked with saffron instantly transport me back to my childhood. For many years I was scared to recreate it, and it took me a long time to perfect the recipe. If you are vegetarian you can omit the meat, but for me, pouring the juices from the lamb over the rice and *tahdig* (crispy base) is literally one of my greatest pleasures.

SERVES 6

olive oil

6 fat garlic cloves, thinly sliced

2¼ cups peeled fresh fava beans

⅓ cup dried dill weed

⅔ stick butter

2½ cups basmati rice

2 to 3 tablespoons ghee (or vegetable oil if you prefer)

½ teaspoon best-quality saffron threads, plus an extra pinch

Maldon sea salt flakes and freshly ground black pepper

For the lamb shanks

vegetable oil

2 onions, halved and thinly sliced into half moons

½ teaspoon Iranian saffron threads, ground to a powder using a mortar and pestle

6 fat garlic cloves, bashed and peeled

4 large lamb shanks

For the lamb shanks, place a large Dutch oven over medium heat, add some vegetable oil, and fry the onions until beginning to soften but not brown. Add the saffron and cook for a few minutes, stirring regularly. Then add the garlic cloves and the lamb shanks along with a generous amount of salt and pepper. Roll the shanks in the onion mixture to coat them, being careful not to let anything brown. Cook for 10 to 15 minutes, turning the shanks over halfway through. Add enough boiling water to cover the shanks, then reduce to medium heat and cook, covered, for 2½ hours until tender and the meat is falling away from the bone. Check the shanks and turn them over occasionally to ensure the meat is submerged, and add more water if necessary.

Meanwhile, heat a large skillet over medium heat, drizzle in some olive oil, and fry the garlic slices until soft. Add the fava beans and dill weed, season heavily with salt and pepper (because you will be seasoning 2½ cups of rice), and then add the butter. Stir and then cook the beans for 10 to 15 minutes. Remove from the heat and set aside.

Bring a separate large saucepan of water to a boil. Add the rice and stir to stop the grains from sticking together, then parboil for about 6 to 7 minutes until the grains turn from a dullish off-white color to a more opaque, brilliant white and have slightly elongated. Drain and immediately rinse thoroughly under cold running water, running your fingers through the rice, until all the grains are well rinsed of starch and completely cooled. Drain the rice thoroughly by shaking the sieve well, then let stand to continue to drain for 10 minutes. Shake off any excess water before use.

Crumple up a large square of parchment paper, then smooth it out and use it to line the bottom of the rice pan (there's no need to line the pan if it is nonstick). Place the pan over very low heat, add the ghee (or vegetable oil), and let the ghee melt. If using a gas stove, pour in ½ inch cold water, and swirl the pan around to mix the ghee (or oil) and water together to prevent the rice from burning (you can omit this if using an electric/induction stove). Season with salt, then loosely scatter just enough rice into the pan to coat the bottom in an even layer. Mix the rest of the rice with the fava-bean mixture, crumble in the saffron, and fold through, then scatter (do not press) the mixture into the pan and spread out to the sides. Using the handle of a wooden spoon, poke lots of holes in the rice, piercing all the way to the bottom of the pan. Wrap the pan lid in a clean dish cloth so that it fits snugly on the pan. If using a gas stove, cook over the lowest flame for 45 minutes. If using an electric/induction stove, cook over medium heat for 1 to 1¼ hours.

Once the rice and lamb are cooked, take the remaining pinch of saffron and crush or grind it in a small bowl. Stir in a teaspoon of boiling water, then add a handful of cooked rice and stir until it turns bright yellow.

Spoon the cooked rice onto a serving platter and scatter it with the handful of saffron-colored rice. Remove the crispy *tahdig* crust from the bottom of the pan, break it up and serve it around the rice.

To serve, you can either break off some of the meat, fold it into the rice, and drizzle it with some of the juice from the shanks, or you can serve the lamb and juices on the side of the rice. I also like to serve this as a soup using the remaining meat juices and some of the rice.

Serve with Burnt Zucchini with Lemon & Feta Yogurt (see page 145).

Afghani Polow

This is a recipe from my childhood that my Afghani Uncle Nehad's mom would make for us when we visited her for lunch. My mom and I always just called it Afghani *polow* (rice), and years later I looked everywhere for a recipe or recreation of the dish in Afghani restaurants only to be told that the one they have is with carrots (and sometimes raisins) and lamb, and is called *ghabboli polow* (a similar recipe for which is in my book *Sirocco*). I have thankfully managed to prize the spice blend that was used to make the rice out of my Aunty Azita, but was otherwise very much left to my own devices to experiment and perfect the recipe. While nothing could ever be as great as the real thing, it's a darned good second, and much as I did when I was a child, my own family loves it!

SERVES 4 TO 6

vegetable oil

2 onions, finely chopped

1¾lb boneless lamb shoulder, cut into
　½-inch cubes

1 heaped teaspoon ground cinnamon

1 teaspoon ground cumin

1 teaspoon ground coriander

½ teaspoon cayenne pepper

¼ teaspoon ground cloves

¼ teaspoon ground nutmeg

6 fat garlic cloves, thinly sliced

⅔ stick butter

3 cups basmati rice

2 to 3 tablespoons ghee
　(or vegetable oil)

Maldon sea salt flakes and freshly
　ground black pepper

Place a saucepan over medium-high heat, pour in a generous amount of vegetable oil, and fry the onions until translucent and beginning to brown around the edges. Add the lamb, spices, and garlic and stir well to coat the meat in the spices, then season heavily with salt and pepper. Cover the pan with a lid but leave a gap open, reduce the heat to low-medium, and cook for an hour, stirring occasionally to stop the mixture from sticking. Remove the lid, add the butter, and increase the heat to reduce any excess liquid so that there is just enough to coat the meat (this should happen pretty quickly because there shouldn't be much liquid anyway), but keep an eye on it and stir occasionally to prevent it from burning. Remove from the heat and set aside.

Bring a large saucepan of water to a boil. Add the rice and stir to stop the grains from sticking together, then parboil for about 6 to 7 minutes until the grains turn from a dullish off-white color to a more opaque, brilliant white and have slightly elongated. Drain and immediately rinse thoroughly under cold running water, running your fingers through the rice, until all the grains are well rinsed of starch and completely cooled. Drain the rice thoroughly by shaking the sieve well, then let stand to continue to drain for 10 minutes. Shake off any excess water before use. Rince the rice saucepan.

continued overleaf

Crumple up a large square of parchment paper, then smooth it out and use it to line the bottom of the rice pan (you can omit this if your pan is nonstick). Place the pan over low-medium heat, add the ghee (or vegetable oil), and let the ghee melt. If using a gas stove, pour in ½ inch cold water, and swirl the pan around to mix the ghee (or oil) and water together to stop the rice from burning (you can omit this if using an electric/induction stove). Season with salt, then loosely scatter just enough rice into the pan to coat the bottom in an even layer. Mix the rest of the rice with the meat mixture, then scatter (do not press) the mixture into the pan and spread out to the sides. Using the handle of a wooden spoon, poke lots of holes in the rice, piercing all the way to the bottom of the pan. Wrap the pan lid in a clean dish cloth so that it fits snugly on the pan. If using a gas stove, cook over the lowest flame for 1 to 1¼ hours. If using an electric/induction stove, cook over medium heat for 2–2½ hours.

Once cooked, remove the lid and spread the rice out to create a flat base. Spoon out the polow into a serving bowl or on a platter. If there is any crispy *tahdig* crust, then serve it on top of the rice.

Serve with Burnt Zucchini with Lemon & Feta Yogurt (see page 145) or Roasted Tomatoes with Labneh & Sumac Spice Oil (see page 177).

Cheat's Zereshk Polow

Zereshk is the Persian word for barberries, those tiny sour red berries that I love and which feature in various recipes of mine. This is the classic recipe that they are used for, albeit a simplified, cheat's version for you to enjoy. This is the version I make the most at home because when the craving hits, I need the speediest solution to curb my appetite. Traditionally the rice would be cooked in the Persian way and served with slow-braised chicken cooked with saffron and onions, but a whole roast chicken or squab is a great choice, too.

SERVES 4

½ teaspoon best-quality saffron threads

1 tablespoon boiling water

1¼ cups basmati rice

2 tablespoons butter

½ cup dried barberries

¼ cup superfine sugar

Maldon sea salt flakes

Using a mortar and pestle, grind the saffron down with some sea salt flakes for abrasion, then transfer to a cup. Add the boiling water, stir, and let stand until required.

Cook the basmati rice in a large saucepan of boiling water following the package directions, making sure not to overcook it. Drain and immediately rinse thoroughly under cold running water, running your fingers through the rice, until all the grains are well rinsed of starch and completely cooled. Drain the rice thoroughly by shaking the sieve well, then let stand for 10 minutes to continue to drain. Shake off any excess water before use.

Melt the butter in a small saucepan over very low heat, add the barberries, and stir them for a minute or two until they begin to plump up. Once they have turned a brighter shade of red, add the sugar and stir until dissolved, then remove immediately from the heat.

Place a generous handful of the cooked rice in a small bowl, pour in the saffron solution, and stir until the grains are all bright orange. Return the rest of the cooked rice to its saucepan over medium heat, then add the barberry and butter mixture and a generous seasoning of salt and mix well. Stir in the saffron-tinted rice, and once everything is hot, pile onto a platter and serve.

Serve with Chicken, Apricot, Orange & Almond Tagine (see page 91) or Ras el Hanout Sticky Spatchcock Squab (see page 118).

Dampokhtak

This is a dish that reminds me of my grandmother, since it was one of the few things she would cook, so I felt compelled to nail this recipe and honor her memory. Ezat Malek, I hope I have made you proud.

SERVES 6 TO 8

2 cups dried split fava beans

2½ cups basmati rice

olive oil

2 large onions, finely chopped

8 garlic cloves, very thinly sliced

¼ stick butter

2 tablespoons ground turmeric

1 cup cold water

2 tablespoons ghee

3 tablespoons Greek yogurt

Maldon sea salt flakes and freshly
    ground black pepper

Soak the dried beans in cold water for 3 hours, then rinse very well, drain, and set aside.

Bring a large saucepan of water to a boil. Add the rice and stir to stop the grains from sticking together, then parboil for about 6 to 7 minutes until the grains turn from a dullish off-white color to a more opaque, brilliant white and have slightly elongated. Drain and immediately rinse thoroughly under cold running water, running your fingers through the rice, until all the grains are well rinsed of starch and completely cooled. Drain the rice thoroughly by shaking the sieve well, then let stand for 10 minutes to continue to drain. Shake off any excess water before use.

Place a large skillet over medium heat, drizzle in enough olive oil to cover the bottom of the pan, and fry the onions until softened. Add the garlic slivers and fry for a couple more minutes. Then add the soaked beans, butter, turmeric, and some pepper and stir well to coat the beans. Pour in the cold water and stir again, then let cook for about 15 minutes, stirring regularly to make sure the beans don't stick. Remove from the heat. (Don't worry that the beans are not fully cooked at this stage.)

Place the rice pan over a low flame if using a gas stove or low-medium heat if using an electric/induction stove. Add the ghee, and once melted, add the yogurt, some salt, and 3 handfuls of the drained rice and mix well. Shake the pan to coat the rice in the yogurt, then pat down to coat the bottom of the pan. Mix the rest of the rice with the bean mixture, scatter (do not press) the mixture into the pan, and spread out to the sides. Using the handle of a wooden spoon, poke lots of holes in the rice, piercing all the way to the bottom of the pan. Wrap the pan lid in a clean dish cloth so that it fits snugly on the pan. If using a gas stove, cook the rice for 45 minutes. If using an electric/induction stove, cook for 1½ hours. Invert or spoon out the rice to serve.

Serve with Roasted Tomatoes with Labneh & Sumac Spice Oil (see page 177).

Creamy Spiced Sausage Pasta,

This is a lovely pasta dish, gently spiced but with so much flavor that it makes it impossible to put down. I love using sausagemeat in pastas because it reminds me of all the wonderful Italian pastas and pizzas I've enjoyed over the years. The sauce is beautifully rich, so a little goes a long way. But then again, I can be terribly greedy and make this batch just for two.

SERVES 3 TO 4

14oz good-quality sausages with a high meat content (flavor of your choice)

1 teaspoon fennel seeds

1 teaspoon cumin seeds

olive oil

4 fat garlic cloves, thinly sliced

2 teaspoons dried wild oregano

2 teaspoons pul biber chile flakes

14oz can diced tomatoes

1 teaspoon superfine sugar

½ cup mascarpone cheese

10½oz pasta shape of your choice (I like spirals and rigatoni tubes)

Maldon sea salt flakes and freshly ground black pepper

grated Parmesan cheese, to serve (optional)

Using a sharp knife, score the sausages and remove the outer casing, then pinch off the sausagemeat into about 6 pieces per sausage.

Heat a large dry saucepan over medium-high heat, add the fennel and cumin seeds, and toast for a couple of minutes until they release their aroma, shaking the pan intermittently to prevent them from burning. Then add a generous drizzle of olive oil and fry the garlic slices until translucent but not colored. Add the sausage pieces and fry for 4 to 5 minutes until sealed and colored all over the outside, shaking the pan to move and roll them over. Next, add the oregano, pul biber, and a generous amount of salt and pepper before adding the tomatoes and sugar and stirring well. Fill the empty tomato can halfway with water, swish it around and pour into the sauce. Reduce the heat to medium and let the sauce simmer for 30 minutes, stirring occasionally. Finally, stir in the mascarpone until evenly incorporated.

Toward the end of the sauce cooking time, cook the pasta in a large saucepan of salted boiling water following the package directions, then drain, reserving some of the cooking water.

Add the pasta to the sauce and toss to coat. Cook for a couple of minutes, then check and taste and adjust the seasoning, if desired, adding a little of the reserved pasta water if you need a bit more liquid. Serve immediately and shower with grated Parmesan if desired. This needs no accompaniment.

Harissa, Tahini & Lamb Spaghetti

By now you will know that I never feel compelled to limit my pasta use to Italian recipes. This is the kind of recipe that comes together pretty easily and is a deeply comforting, spiced bowl of spaghetti with all the familiarity of a good meat-and-spaghetti combo but with wildly different flavors. I don't like using the word "fusion" because it infers intent to purposely blend one thing into another. All I know is this kind of food tastes great to me and has notes that hit every spot on my satisfaction scale. If you feel like making your noodles a little more soupy, simply add more of the pasta cooking water or a light vegetable stock to increase the final volume of liquid.

SERVES 4

vegetable oil

1 large onion, finely chopped

6 fat garlic cloves, finely sliced

1lb 2oz ground lamb

1 tablespoon garlic granules

1 tablespoon curry powder

1 tablespoon ground cumin

2 tablespoons rose harissa

3 tablespoons tahini

3 tablespoons light soy sauce

10½oz spaghetti

4 scallions, finely sliced diagonally from root to tip

2 tablespoons toasted sesame seeds

Maldon sea salt flakes and freshly ground black pepper

Place a large skillet over medium-high heat, add a drizzle of vegetable oil, and fry the onion until soft and translucent, then stir in the garlic slices and cook for 2 minutes to soften. Add the ground lamb and immediately break it up as finely as possible to stop it from cooking in clumps, then stir in the garlic granules and dry spices until incorporated into the meat. Continue cooking, stirring as you go. Add the harissa, tahini, soy sauce, and salt and pepper. Stir everything together until evenly combined.

Cook the spaghetti in a large saucepan of salted boiling water following the package directions, then drain, reserving some of the cooking water.

Add the spaghetti to the lamb mixture and mix well, then pour in enough of the reserved pasta water to make the mixture a little soupy. Finally, add the scallions and sesame seeds, mix together, and serve scattered with the chopped cilantro. This needs no accompaniment.

Punchy Bell Pepper, Tomato & Pasta Soup

When I think of soups, I think of my mother. I'd like to tell you a fondly recalled tale about how she always made soups for me when I was growing up and they were the best I'd ever tasted, but the truth is, beyond opening a can and reheating its contents, my mother has never made a soup from scratch in her life. However, she loves soup more than most people do. This recipe relies heavily on kitchen-cupboard ingredients for its flavor. It's lovely and punchy, and the orzo pasta makes it more of a meal than just a soup.

SERVES 4

olive oil

1 large onion, finely chopped

¼ cup tomato paste

4 fat garlic cloves, thinly sliced

1 green bell pepper, cored, seeded, and halved, then cut widthwise into thin strips

1 tablespoon dried wild oregano

1 tablespoon dried mint

1 teaspoon pul biber chile flakes

⅓ cup orzo pasta

2 tablespoons butter (optional)

1 quart boiling water

4 scallions, thinly sliced from root to tip

Maldon sea salt flakes and freshly ground black pepper

Place a medium saucepan over medium-high heat, drizzle in enough olive oil to just coat the bottom, and fry the onion until translucent and beginning to color around the edges.

Mix the tomato paste into the onion and cook for a few minutes, stirring regularly to ensure it doesn't stick. Add the garlic, green bell pepper, herbs, pul biber, and a generous amount of salt and pepper and cook, stirring well, for a couple of minutes.

Add the orzo and butter (or a drizzle of olive oil for a vegan option) and stir well to coat the orzo and ensure everything is evenly combined. Cook for 4 to 5 minutes, stirring to prevent the mixture from sticking. Add the boiling water, stir, and cook over medium heat for 25 to 30 minutes, stirring occasionally, until the orzo is cooked and the soup has reduced nicely.

Stir in the scallions, then taste and adjust the seasoning if desired. This needs no accompaniment.

Nut Butter Noodles

I first came across peanut noodles thanks to the great Nigella Lawson, whose recipes have provided me with so much satisfaction and inspiration over the years. Nigella knows good food and introduced many of us to the art of being a home cook, making it undaunting and accessible in a way that nobody had quite managed to do before her. This dish switches it up with the addition of coconut milk and garlic and, of course, also features nigella seeds. Credit where credit is due, Nigella continues to inspire me, and I make her recipes at home more than anybody else's. This dish is best eaten as soon as it has been made.

SERVES 4 TO 6

7oz medium egg noodles

2 tablespoons sesame seeds

⅓ cup crunchy peanut butter

2 tablespoons soy sauce

2 tablespoons superfine sugar

1 cup coconut milk

2 garlic cloves, minced

juice of ½ lime

Maldon sea salt flakes and freshly
   ground black pepper

To serve

½ teaspoon nigella seeds

1 teaspoon pul biber chile flakes

5 scallions, thinly sliced diagonally
   from root to tip

good handful of fresh cilantro leaves

Cook the noodles following the package directions, then drain, rinse in cold water, drain again, and set aside.

Heat a dry skillet over medium heat, add the sesame seeds, and toast for a few minutes until nicely golden brown. Remove from the pan and set aside.

Place a small saucepan over low-medium heat, add the peanut butter, soy sauce, sugar, coconut milk, garlic, and lime juice mix well. Season with salt and pepper and heat through until hot but not bubbling. If the mixture is too thick, thin it down with some water or milk.

Pour the warm peanut sauce over the noodles and then toss with the toasted sesame seeds. Serve on a flat plate, scattered with the nigella seeds, pul biber, scallions, and cilantro, and eat immediately. (As delicious as it is, once cold it will set and need warming through to revive it.)

Serve with Tamarind Chicken Wings (see page 65) or Cod Flavor Bombs (see page 77).

Spiced Chicken, Coconut & Noodle Stew

Coconut is one of my favorite flavors. From fresh coconut and desiccated to juice and coconut milk, I love all forms. I find the addition of coconut improves most things, but I especially like it in soups and curries. Though this is not a curry, this warming and fragrant stew offers many of the same properties.

The addition of noodles reminds me of the famous *khao soi* dish of Northern Thailand and makes this more of a meal, though you can omit the noodles and simply serve it with rice or naan bread.

SERVES 4

vegetable oil

2 onions, coarsely chopped

1¼lb boneless, skinless chicken thighs

4 green cardamom pods,
 lightly crushed

1 teaspoon cumin seeds

2 teaspoons ground turmeric

2 tablespoons rose harissa

14fl oz can coconut milk

10½oz medium egg noodles

Maldon sea salt flakes and freshly
 ground black pepper

To serve (optional)

handful of bean sprouts

lime wedges

chopped fresh cilantro leaves

Place a large saucepan over medium-high heat, drizzle in some vegetable oil, and fry the onions until softened and translucent. Add the chicken and dry spices along with a generous amount of salt and pepper. Roll the chicken over to coat it in the onion and spice mixture, then stir-fry for a few minutes. Add the harissa and stir-fry for a few more minutes.

Reduce the heat to medium so the mixture simmers gently. Pour in the coconut milk and enough water to just about cover the chicken, and stir to combine. Then cover the pan with a lid and cook on low heat for an hour, stirring occasionally to prevent the mixture from sticking. Keep an eye on the liquid volume. You want to ensure that the chicken is cooked and tender but also that there is a lovely soupy, creamy broth.

When the stew is ready, cook the noodles following the package directions, then drain and divide between 4 serving bowls.

To serve, pour the stew over the cooked noodles, then add the bean sprouts, lime wedges and cilantro if desired. This needs no accompaniment.

Mushroom Spaghetti with Creamy Pistachio & Garlic Sauce

Tahini is invaluable in the kitchen, and brilliant for creating rich, creamy textures in recipes without the need for dairy or meat. Having once had to temporarily cut out both meat and dairy, I was desperate for something that would satisfy me in a way that a comforting creamy pasta would do, and so this recipe was born. Despite being back to my normal eating regimen, I still absolutely love this rich, creamy, and delicious recipe.

SERVES 4

1lb 2oz cremino mushrooms, quartered

vegetable oil

10½oz spaghetti

For the sauce

⅔ cup pistachio nuts

2 fat garlic cloves, peeled

⅔ cup warm water, or more if needed

2 tablespoons tahini

Maldon sea salt flakes and freshly ground black pepper

Heat a large skillet or saucepan over high heat, and once hot, add the mushrooms to the dry pan. Let them release their liquid and then cook until all the liquid has evaporated. Add a drizzle of oil, then fry until nicely browned in parts, stirring occasionally. Remove the pan from the heat and set aside.

Put all the sauce ingredients into a bullet blender or mini food processor and blitz until as smooth as possible, adding a little more warm water if needed to make the mixture loose enough to blitz.

Cook the spaghetti in a large saucepan of salted boiling water following the package directions, then drain, reserving some of the cooking water.

Reheat the mushrooms over medium-high heat and add the sauce, stirring to coat the mushrooms. Taste and adjust the seasoning if desired, then cook the sauce for a couple of minutes. Add the spaghetti and some of the reserved pasta water to the mushroom pan and mix well until the sauce and mushrooms evenly coat the pasta. Add a little more pasta water if needed and some more seasoning to taste, then serve immediately. This needs no accompaniment.

Soup e Jow

My mother adores this Persian soup so much that she begged me to learn how to make it. I did, and now it's a house staple that everyone enjoys. Even though it is incredibly simple, it's really quite comforting, which in my humble opinion is what all the best soups should be. *Jow* is the Persian word for "barley," and I like to go heavy on the barley because I love the texture once cooked. The final flourish comes from lemon juice, something Persians are obsessed with adding to everything. I will leave this element up to you, but a little lemon does work well with it.

SERVES 3 TO 4

olive oil

1 large onion, finely chopped

1 large carrot, peeled and very finely diced

2 tablespoons butter

1 tablespoon garlic granules

3 tablespoons all-purpose flour

3 cups whole or 2% milk
(but not nonfat)

¾ cup pearl barley

1 quart boiling water

juice of ½ lemon, or to taste

1 tablespoon dried chives (optional)

Maldon sea salt flakes and freshly
ground black pepper

Place a large saucepan over medium heat, drizzle in some olive oil, and fry the onion and carrot until soft but not colored. Add the butter, garlic granules, and a generous amount of salt and pepper. Once the butter has melted, stir in the flour quickly to avoid lumps. Add some of the milk and work the flour paste into it until smooth. Keep adding milk and working in the flour paste until it is evenly combined.

Add the barley, boiling water, and any remaining milk. Stir the mixture really well and cook the soup over low-medium heat for 45 minutes or so, stirring occasionally, until the barley is soft and puffed up. Taste and adjust the seasoning, if desired, and add more liquid if you want to, then stir in the lemon juice to taste. Finally, add the dried chives, if desired, and cook for a few more minutes until they are bright green and soft, then serve. This needs no accompaniment.

Samosa Pasta

I absolutely love lamb samosas. The spicy filling with occasional sweet bursts of peas, and the ratio of meat to wonderful crisp pastry is literally one of the world's best inventions. But I have often wondered what combining that kind of filling with pasta would taste like, and it's really rather good, I can tell you. We love it in my household, and even though I pack in the spices, the kids love it, too, because, well, they have good taste in food. It's a really simple recipe to make using peas from the freezer and spices and pasta from the cupboards together with some ground beef. It's perfect midweek supper food.

SERVES 3 TO 4

vegetable oil

1 large onion, finely chopped

9oz ground beef

1 heaped teaspoon garlic granules

1 teaspoon cumin seeds

1 teaspoon ground cinnamon

1 teaspoon ground turmeric

1 teaspoon dried red chile flakes

3 tablespoons tomato paste

1 cup warm water

3 handfuls of frozen peas

9oz farfalle pasta (or pasta shape of your choice)

1 small pack (about 1oz) of fresh cilantro, coarsely chopped

Maldon sea salt flakes and freshly ground black pepper

Place a large skillet over medium-high heat, drizzle in some vegetable oil, and fry the onion until nicely browned. Add the ground beef and immediately break it up as finely as you can to prevent it from cooking in clumps. Then add the garlic granules, all the spices, the tomato paste, and a generous amount of salt and pepper. Stir-fry the ground beef for a few minutes. Pour in the warm water and stir-fry again until mostly evaporated. Lastly, stir in the peas and then turn the heat off.

Cook the pasta in a large saucepan of salted boiling water following the package directions, then drain, reserving a cup of the cooking water. Add the pasta to the spicy beef mixture and place over medium-high heat. Pour in the reserved pasta water and mix together well. Taste and adjust the seasoning if desired, then add the cilantro, stir through, and serve. This needs no accompaniment.

Spiced Eggplant & Tomato Pasta

Years ago, I learned of a Southern Italian recipe called *melanzane a funghetto* (eggplant fried in strips, then cooked in a simple tomato sauce with a little garlic). Although utterly delicious in its simplicity, over time my version has evolved with the addition of whole spices and a gentle burst of chile heat, which sits a little more comfortably in my Middle Eastern repertoire and makes for a fantastic pasta dish.

SERVES 4 TO 5

3 large eggplants, peeled and cut into batons ½ inch in thickness and 2 to 2½ inches in length

olive oil

1 teaspoon cumin seeds

1 teaspoon fennel seeds

1 head of garlic, cloves separated and thinly sliced

10½oz baby plum or small tomatoes, halved

2 teaspoons pul biber chile flakes

1 heaped teaspoon garlic granules

14oz can diced tomatoes

2 teaspoons superfine sugar

14oz spaghetti

Maldon sea salt flakes and freshly ground black pepper

Parmesan-style vegetarian or vegan cheese to serve (optional)

Preheat the oven to 400°F. Line your largest baking pan with parchment paper.

Arrange the eggplant batons on the lined pan in a single layer, drizzle generously with olive oil, and roast for 35 to 40 minutes until nicely browned all over but not dried out.

Meanwhile, heat a large dry skillet or saucepan over medium heat, add the cumin and fennel seeds, and toast for a couple of minutes. Then drizzle in enough olive oil to coat the bottom. Add the garlic slices and fry for a couple of minutes until softened and translucent. Add the fresh tomatoes, pul biber, garlic granules, and a generous amount of salt and pepper. Stir to combine really well, then cook for a few minutes. Add the diced tomatoes and sugar and stir well. Fill the empty tomato can with water, pour into the sauce, and stir again. Then let simmer for about 30 minutes until nicely thickened.

Once the eggplant batons are done, remove from the oven and set aside. Taste the sauce and adjust the seasoning if desired, then stir in the roasted eggplant batons.

Cook the spaghetti in a large saucepan of salted boiling water following the package directions, then drain, reserving some of the cooking water. Add the spaghetti to the sauce and toss to coat, adding a little of the reserved pasta water, if needed, to emulsify the mixture. Serve immediately, with grated vegetarian cheese on top if desired. This needs no accompaniment.

Sweet

Apple Fritters with Cinnamon Sugar

I must confess, I am not the biggest fan of frying things unless it is absolutely worth the end result. These apple fritters are most definitely worth it. How can a handful of ingredients create such joy? Trust me, they do. Needless to say, you can substitute the apples with bananas or mix and match, but I really do like the texture and burst of sweetness that comes from using apples, and cinnamon seems to be the perfect partner for them, too.

SERVES 4

¾ cup all-purpose flour

2 teaspoons baking powder

½ cup cold water

vegetable oil, or frying

2 apples

For the cinnamon sugar

⅓ cup superfine sugar

2 teaspoons ground cinnamon

Mix the sugar and cinnamon together in a small bowl.

Mix the flour and baking powder together in a mixing bowl. Using a wire whisk, gradually beat in the cold water gently until you have a smooth batter but without overbeating (otherwise the batter will be heavy).

Heat a large, deep skillet over medium-high heat, pour in about 1 inch of vegetable oil, and bring to frying temperature. (Add a little bit of the batter. If it sizzles immediately, the oil is hot enough.) Line a plate with a double layer of paper towels.

Meanwhile, peel and core the apples, then cut them into slices ¼ inch in thickness.

Dip each apple slice in turn into the batter and shake off any excess, then carefully lower them into the hot oil and fry in batches, 5 to 6 slices at a time depending on the size of your pan, for about a minute on each side until the batter has puffed up and turned golden brown all over. Remove with a slotted spoon and transfer to the paper-lined plate to drain. While still hot, coat the fritters in the cinnamon sugar and serve.

Cinnamon Brioche Toast

The first time I tried Shibuya honey toast in Bangkok, I was completely smitten. It's very much a sweet treat of Japanese origin, and I find that there is much to love about a cube of buttered and sugared pillowy white bread, pan-fried until crispy, smothered in more butter, and drowned in honey with a scoop of vanilla ice cream on top. Although this quick and easy dessert/breakfast dish is inspired by Shibuya toast, it's much simpler and yet every bit as satisfying. If the cinnamon sugar exterior doesn't provide you with enough indulgence, a scoop of whipped vanilla cream may just help seal the deal.

MAKES 4

3 tablespoons superfine sugar

1 heaped teaspoon ground cinnamon, plus extra to decorate

½ stick butter, softened

4 slices of brioche loaf, about 1 inch in thickness

For the vanilla cream (optional)

⅔ cup heavy cream

1 teaspoon vanilla bean paste

If making the vanilla cream, whip the cream to soft peak stage, then stir in the vanilla paste. Set aside in the refrigerator while you cook the brioche toast.

Mix the sugar and cinnamon together in a small bowl.

Heat a large skillet over medium heat (low-medium if using a gas stove).

Butter each slice of brioche on both sides. Take half the cinnamon sugar and sprinkle it on top of the 4 slices, patting it into the butter.

Once the skillet is hot, place the brioche in it, sugar-side down. Add the remaining cinnamon sugar to the 4 slices, again patting it into the butter. Fry the slices for a couple of minutes on each side, checking that the sugar has caramelized on both sides.

Carefully transfer the brioche slices from the skillet to serving plates. Once the sugar cools, it will firm up on the brioche to form a lovely crunchy crust. Serve with the whipped vanilla cream sprinkled with extra ground cinnamon if desired.

Feta, Basil & Strawberry Cheesecake Cups

I like to think of myself as a slightly wacky creator of desserts—nothing too complicated because I'm lazy, but now and again I like to put together something unusual that I know you will all enjoy. This is one such recipe. The feta element is inspired by my love for Honey & Co.'s feta and honey cheesecake. This is quite different, but I wanted to reference my lovely friends Sarit and Itamar because they are endlessly inspiring. I love combining fruit with herbs and this combination of flavors is a knockout. Don't believe me? Try it!

MAKES 4

½ stick unsalted butter, melted

1 cup graham cracker crumbs

1 cup finely crumbled feta cheese

1 cup full-fat cream cheese

⅓ cup superfine sugar, plus 1 tablespoon

⅔ cup heavy cream

¼ cup finely chopped basil leaves
    plus a few whole leaves, to decorate

2¼ cups strawberries, hulled, divided

squeeze of lemon juice

Mix the melted butter with the graham cracker crumbs in a mixing bowl until evenly combined.

Add the feta to another mixing bowl, then add the cream cheese and, using a hand-held electric mixer, beat together until as smooth as possible. Add the ⅓ cup sugar and beat it in, then pour in the cream and add the chopped basil. Beat the mixture for a couple of minutes until evenly combined.

Blitz ½ cup of the strawberries with the tablespoon of sugar and lemon juice in a blender until liquidized. Finely dice the remaining strawberries and stir them into the strawberry mixture.

Divide the crumb mixture between 4 glass tumblers and press down to flatten and create a crust. Spoon an equal quantity of the cheesecake mixture evenly onto each crust, then top with an equal quantity of the strawberry mixture. Refrigerate for at least 2 hours or overnight before serving.

Lime, Coconut & Cardamom Loaf Cake

This is a wonderful combination of flavors and a highly satisfying treat. The sponge cake itself has the pleasing chewiness that I adore in cakes courtesy of the desiccated coconut, and the frosting gives a lovely extra hit of coconut and lime for the finish. For a real afternoon delight, I love a slice with a nice cup of my favorite Yorkshire tea. The leftover coconut milk makes a fantastic addition to soups, curries, and stews or even smoothies. Keep in the refrigerator and use within 24 hours, or freeze in ice-cube trays until needed.

SERVES 6 TO 8

3 eggs

⅔ cup superfine sugar

finely grated zest of 2 unwaxed limes, some reserved for decorating, and juice of 1

seeds from 6 green cardamom pods, ground using a mortar and pestle

1 teaspoon vanilla extract

½ cup desiccated coconut

14fl oz can coconut milk, solidified cream on top spooned off, leaving the liquid unused, divided

1¼ cups all-purpose flour

1 teaspoon baking powder

½ stick unsalted butter, melted

¾ cup confectioners' sugar, sifted, plus more if needed

handful of coconut flakes

Preheat the oven to 350°F. Line a 2-pound (9-inch) loaf pan with a nonstick paper liner, or cut a rectangle of parchment paper, crumple it up, then smooth it out and use it to line the pan.

Put the eggs, superfine sugar, lime zest and half the juice, the cardamom, vanilla, desiccated coconut, and 3 level tablespoons of the coconut cream into a mixing bowl. Use a wooden spoon to beat it together until evenly combined. Add the flour, baking powder, and melted butter and stir until smooth.

Pour the batter into the lined pan and bake for 1 hour, or until a skewer or knife inserted into the center comes out clean. Remove from the oven and let cool in the pan.

Meanwhile, to make the frosting, put the remaining coconut cream and lime juice into a bowl and beat in the confectioners' sugar until smooth. Depending on the volume of lime juice, you may need to add a bit more.

Transfer the cooled cake to a wire rack. Spread the frosting over the top, scatter with the reserved lime zest and coconut flakes, and then let stand to cool completely. Cut into slices to serve.

Pistachio & Chocolate Dream Cake

This is the cake of my dreams, combining pistachios with chocolate in the most indulgent and spectacular way. There really is little I can add here because you will see what I mean when you make it.

SERVES 8

1¾ sticks butter, softened, plus extra for greasing

¾ cup superfine sugar

1 teaspoon vanilla extract

4 large eggs

1½ cups all-purpose flour

2 teaspoons baking powder

1½ cups pistachio slivers (or coarsely chopped whole nuts), very finely ground in a food processor, divided

½ cup milk

For the frosting

1¾ sticks unsalted butter, softened

2¾ cups confectioners' sugar

¾ cup unsweetened cocoa powder

1 heaped teaspoon vanilla bean paste

½ cup heavy cream

pinch of Maldon sea salt flakes

Preheat the oven to 350°F. Grease the insides of two 8-inch round cake pans with butter. Cut 2 disks of parchment paper to fit inside the bottom of the pans. Crumple up the paper disks, smooth them out, and then use one to line the bottom of each pan.

Using an electric hand-held mixer, beat the butter, sugar, and vanilla extract together in a large mixing bowl until light and fluffy. Then add the eggs and beat again until incorporated. Next, add the flour, baking powder, and half of the ground pistachios and beat until smooth. Gradually pour in the milk, beating until completely incorporated and the batter is nice and loose.

Divide the batter between the prepared pans and bake for 30 minutes, or until a skewer inserted into the center comes out clean. Remove from the oven, let stand for 5 minutes, then invert the cakes onto a wire rack. Remove the parchment paper and let cool.

To make the frosting, place all the ingredients in a large bowl and use an electric hand-held mixer or stand mixer to beat together until smooth. Spread one-third of the frosting on top of one cake and scatter with one-third of the remaining ground pistachios. Set the second cake on top and use the remaining frosting to coat the top and sides. Scatter with the remaining pistachios and serve. In warmer weather, you may wish to refrigerate the cake for an hour before serving.

Raspberry & Pistachio Crêpe Cake

I have chosen this particular combination as I simply adore pistachios with raspberries. And with the help of a little natural food coloring, this little creation looks (and tastes) very special indeed.

SERVES 6

¾ cup all-purpose flour, sifted

pinch of salt

2 eggs

1 cup milk

3 tablespoons water

½ stick butter, melted,
   plus 3 tablespoons,
   melted, for frying

1 heaped tablespoon superfine sugar

For the filling

3¾ cups heavy cream

⅓ cup confectioners' sugar

2 teaspoons vanilla bean paste

pink natural food coloring

½ cup pistachio slivers (or coarsely
   chopped whole nuts), very finely
   ground in a food processor

2 cups raspberries

To make the crêpe batter, put the flour, salt, and eggs into a large mixing bowl. Mix the milk and water together in a small pitcher, then whisk into the flour mixture a little at a time using either a fork or an electric hand mixer to beat out any lumps. Mix in the ½ stick melted butter and the superfine sugar and set aside.

Heat a large skillet over medium-high heat. Drizzle in 1 teaspoon melted butter and tilt the pan to spread it around the bottom of the pan. Quickly pour in just enough crêpe batter to barely coat the bottom (you want a thin crêpe, not a pancake) and tilt the pan to spread the batter evenly to make about an 8-inch crêpe. Cook for 1 minute, or until the edges start to curl up and the underside is golden, then flip or turn the crêpe over with a spatula and cook for a further 30 seconds or so until golden brown on the other side. Transfer the crêpe to a plate and cover with a sheet of parchment paper. Repeat with the remaining batter to make 8 crêpes in total, adding 1 teaspoon melted butter to the pan each time and stacking the cooked crêpes on the plate with parchment paper in between each. Let cool, cover, and chill in the refrigerator until ready to assemble the cake.

To make the filling, mix the cream with the confectioners' sugar and vanilla bean paste in a large mixing bowl, then add some pink food coloring, a little at a time, until you reach the desired color (some brands need more, some less). Using an electric hand mixer, whip the cream mixture until stiff, pillowy peaks form.

To assemble the cake, remove the crêpes from the refrigerator and place 1 on a serving plate. Spread it with enough cream mixture to cover the surface. Place another crêpe on top and repeat until you have added the last one. Cover the top and exposed edges of the cake with the remaining cream mixture, then scatter with the pistachios followed by the raspberries. Let chill in the refrigerator for an hour to firm up before serving.

Sticky Coffee & Spice Cake

Sticky toffee pudding is among the UK's favorite desserts, and a firm family favorite, too. There really is no messing with perfection, but this version, inspired by the aromatic cardamom-spiked coffees I drank in Dubai, is worth a try. The combination is so good I used it as a rich toffee-like sauce over a springy sponge cake to create a lovely, more grown-up recipe that makes a warming, spiced dessert after an Eastern feast.

SERVES 9

For the cake

1 stick butter, softened, plus extra
   for greasing

3 eggs

1 cup light brown sugar

2 cups all-purpose flour

1 teaspoon baking powder

1 teaspoon baking soda

1¼ cups milk

vanilla ice cream, to serve

For the coffee & spice sauce

seeds from 6 cardamom pods, finely
   ground using a mortar and pestle

½ teaspoon ground cinnamon

3 teaspoons coffee granules, dissolved
   in 2 tablespoons boiling water

¾ cup light brown sugar

1 teaspoon vanilla bean paste

1 tablespoon molasses

¾ stick butter

1¼ cups heavy cream

Preheat the oven to 350°F. Grease a nonstick 8-inch square cake pan with butter.

Put all the ingredients for the cake into a mixing bowl and beat together until well combined. Pour the batter into the greased pan and bake for 45 minutes, or until a skewer inserted into the center comes out clean.

Meanwhile, stir all the sauce ingredients together in a saucepan and cook over low heat until the sugar has dissolved and the sauce is smooth. Increase the heat and bring to a rolling boil for 1 to 2 minutes, then stir well and remove from the heat.

Remove the cake from the oven, then slice into squares and serve with the sauce poured over it, and topped with a scoop of vanilla ice cream.

Tahini, Almond & Chocolate Crumble Cookies

I cannot tell you how satisfying these cookies are, so much so that I usually have a bag of the cookie dough balls stashed in my freezer ready for baking whenever the craving hits. The texture is crumbly in an almost sandy way. The absolute optimum time to enjoy them is 30 minutes out of the oven, when the cookies have cooled down but the chocolate is still gooey. They are also great the next day provided you've stored them in an airtight container overnight, and are perfect for sharing (or not, if you're anything like me).

MAKES 14

1 stick butter, softened

⅔ cup soft light brown sugar

⅓ cup superfine sugar

½ teaspoon ground cinnamon

⅓ cup tahini (use the solids and avoid the oil as much as possible)

1¼ cups all-purpose flour

½ teaspoon baking powder

½ teaspoon baking soda

⅓ cup coarsely chopped blanched almonds

7oz dark chocolate chunks (70% cocoa solids)

Beat the softened butter, sugars, and cinnamon together in a mixing bowl until light and fluffy. Then add the tahini and mix until smooth. Next, add the flour, baking powder, and baking soda and stir until evenly combined. Finally, add the almonds and dark chocolate chunks and mix until evenly distributed.

Divide the cookie dough into 14 equal portions and form each into a ball. Chill in the refrigerator for at least 4 hours, or overnight if preferred. Once chilled, you can then freeze the cookie dough balls for later use.

To bake, preheat the oven to 350°F. Line a cookie sheet with parchment paper.

Place your dough balls, well spaced out, on the lined cookie sheet and gently flatten them (omit this stage if using frozen dough). Bake for 16 minutes (or 18 from frozen). Remove from the oven and let cool on the cookie sheet for 30 minutes, then enjoy.

Tea, Cranberry, Orange & Macadamia Shortbread Cookies

I have loved shortbread cookies ever since I was a kid and I always thought it must be pretty difficult to make, but the best things in life (and food) usually tend to be very simple. Happily, shortbread cookies prove to be no exception. It's also very versatile when it comes to flavor additions, with this particular combination being a standout winner for me. These cookies will also make lovely gifts for deserving friends and loved ones. Even though they keep well once baked, you can also halve the shortbread dough and freeze half for later use, then defrost, and keep in the refrigerator until you're ready to bake.

MAKES 18 TO 20

2 Earl Grey tea bags

2½ cups all-purpose flour

¾ cup confectioners' sugar

⅔ cup macadamia nuts or blanched almonds, coarsely chopped

¾ cup dried cranberries, coarsely chopped

finely grated zest of 2 unwaxed oranges

1 teaspoon vanilla bean paste

pinch of salt

1¾ sticks unsalted butter, softened

olive oil

superfine sugar, for sprinkling

Split open the teabags and tip the tea into a large mixing bowl with the flour, confectioners' sugar, nuts, cranberries, orange zest, vanilla, and salt and stir to combine. Add the butter and just enough olive oil to work the mixture with your hands into an evenly combined ball of firm dough.

Roll the dough into a log about 1½ to 2 inches in diameter. Seal securely in plastic wrap and twist the ends to encase the dough tightly, like a candy wrapper. Chill in the refrigerator for at least an hour or overnight.

Preheat the oven to 300°F. Line a large cookie sheet with parchment paper.

Unwrap the dough, cut into disks ½ an inch in thickness, and place on the lined cookie sheet, about ¾ of an inch apart, then sprinkle liberally with superfine sugar. Bake for 20 minutes, or until the edges turn slightly golden.

Remove from the oven and let cool on the cookie sheet (this allows the cookies to firm up). Once completely cool, they are ready to enjoy.

Index

A

almonds 17, 30, 91, 233
apple, fritters 218–19
apricots 90–1, 107, 118
arugula 18
avocado & halloumi wraps 84–5

B

bacon, sublime BHT 70–1
barberries, dried 96, 107, 133, 149,
    195
beans, black 33
beans, borlotti 34–5
beans, cannellini 33, 82, 141, 178
beans, red kidney 141
beef
    cucumber & herb salad 36–7
    one pan ground beef 100–1
    & potato stew, spiced 114–15
    samosa pasta 212–13
    spicy keema rolls 72–3
beet & pomegranate salad
    12–13
Belgian endive 44–5
bell peppers
    bean & thyme khorak 141
    couscous salad 10
    halloumi skewers 162
    roasted vegetable & bean salad
        32–3
    spiced & soupy seafood 134–5
    sticky lamb with harissa 104
    tavuk güveç 128–9
    tomato & harissa sauce 166
    & tomato pasta soup 202–3
    vegetable layers, baked 138–9
bhaji buns 156–7
börek
    carrot, oregano & feta 50–1
    ground lamb 102–3
    mushroom cigar 68–9, 73
bread
    bhaji buns 156–7
    cinnamon brioche toast 220–1
    roasted vegetable & labneh
        tartines 81
broccoli 154–5
broccolini 40–1
butter
    barberry 133
    mint 92
    spiced 169
buttermilk 99
butternut squash 30–1

C

cabbage 146–8, 152–3
cake
    lime coconut & cardamom 225
    pistachio & chocolate 226–7
    raspberry & pistachio crêpe 228–9
    sticky coffee & spice 230–1
carrots 50–1, 121, 149–51, 211
cauliflower & lentil salad 16–17
celery root 149–51
cheese
    lamb & Cheddar tortillas 66–7
    & potato puffs 54–5
    see also feta; halloumi
cheesecake, strawberry cups 222
chicken
    apricot, orange & almond tagine
        90–1
    kid's chicken korma 130–1
    ras el hanout sticky spatchcock
        squab 118–19
    shawarma salad 14–15
    spiced coconut stew 206–7
    tamarind wings 64–5
    tavuk güveç 128–9
    tender TFC 98–9
chickpeas
    couscous salad 10
    dream platter 20–1
    & eggplants, oven-baked 174–5
    feta & barberry pie 149–51
    & sweet potato balls 86–7
    torsh e shami 117
chiles, pickled 154
chocolate 226–7, 232–3
cinnamon sugar 218, 221
coconut milk 114, 130, 204, 207,
    225
cod, flavor bombs 76–7
coffee & spice cake 230–1
cookies, tahini almond & chocolate
    232–3
corn on the cob 99
couscous salad 10–11
cranberries, dried 30, 234
cream cheese 222
cucumber
    beef & herb salad 36–7
    dream platter 20–1
    halloumi & nectarine salad
        24–5
    pickled 14
    in sabich 74
curry powder 38, 54, 130–1

D

dampokhtak 196–7
dates, in salad 17
dolma, cabbage "bowl" 146–8

dumplings, lamb & cilantro 60–1

E

eggplant
    & chickpeas, oven-baked 174–5
    & ground beef 100–1
    honey-roasted, with spiced
        tahini 170–1
    Mama Ghanoush 158–9
    pomegranate & tomato
        184–5
    with ras el hanout & lamb rib
        chops 109
    roasted vegetable & bean salad
        32–3
    roasted vegetable & labneh
        tartines 81
    sabich 74–5
    smoked, with lime & maple
        dressing 142–3
    with spicy peanut sauce 172–3
    sweet, spicy & crunchy 182–3
    tahchin 125
    & tomato spicy pasta 214–15
    vegetable layers, baked 138–9

eggs
    in dream platter 20–1
    Nargessi kofta loaf 107
    nimroo mirzai 160–1
    with potatoes & spinach, fried
        168–9
    in sabich 74

F

fatayer puffs 56–7
fava beans 189, 196–7

feta
    basil & strawberry cheesecake
        cups 222–3
    & bean patties 82–3
    carrot & oregano börek 50–1
    dream platter 21
    & herb balls 62–3
    lemon yogurt & zucchini 145
    root vegetable & barberry pie
        149–51
    & tomato fritters 180–1
    torsh e shami 117
    vegetable layers, baked 138–9
    zucchini, lemon & pine nut tart
        52–3
figs, dried 96
filo pastry 50, 58, 69, 73, 103, 149
fritters
    apple 218–19
    spicy shrimp 78–9
    tomato & feta 180–1

H

halloumi
    airbags 58–9
    & avocado wraps 84–5
    couscous salad 10
    marinated skewers 162–3
    nectarine & cucumber salad 24–5
    orange & pistachio arugula salad
        18–19
    sublime BHT 70–1
harissa
    broccolini & rice salad 41
    coconut chicken stew 206
    crispy, sticky lamb 104
    ketchup 70, 85
    one pan ground beef 100

spiced lamb & potato stew 114
spiced & soupy seafood 134–5
spicy peanut sauce 173
sweet & spicy sauce 182
& tahini lamb spaghetti 200–1
tomato & bell pepper sauce 166
yogurt 66, 86
hummus salad 22–3

K

khorak 140–1
koftas, lamb 92–3
    Nargessi kofta loaf 106–7

L

labneh 81
    with roasted tomatoes 177
lamb
    Afghani polow 191–3
    börek 102–3
    butterflied, with tahini garlic
        yogurt 122–4
    & Cheddar tortillas 66–7
    chops, marinated 94–5
    & cilantro dumplings 60–1
    crispy, sticky harissa 104–5
    fatayer puffs 56–7
    fig & lemon tagine 96–7
    harissa & tahini spaghetti 200
    herb koftas 92–3
    Nargessi kofta loaf 106–7
    Persian dolmeh e barg
        111–13
    & potato stew, spiced 114–15
    rib chops with ras el hanout &
        orange 108–10
    shanks, & baghala polow
        188–90
    taas kabab 120–1

tahchin 125

torsh e shami 117

lemons, preserved 22, 96, 154

lentil & cauliflower salad 16–17

lettuce 14

lime

coconut & cardamom loaf 225

dried 95

M

macadamia nuts 234

mascarpone cheese 198

measurements 4

mushroom

cigar börek 68–9

salad 28–9

spaghetti, with pistachio &
garlic sauce 208–9

mussels, spiced & soupy
134–5

N

nectarines 24–5

nigella seeds 54, 62, 69, 204

nimroo mirzai 160–1

noodles

& coconut chicken stew 206–7

nut butter 204–5

shrimp, orange & pomegranate
vermicelli salad 46–7

O

olives 10, 21, 26

onion bhaji buns 156–7

orange

chicken, apricot & almond
tagine 90–1

halloumi & pistachio arugula

salad 18–19

with ras el hanout & lamb rib
chops 109

shrimp vermicelli salad 46

shortbread cookies 234–5

P

parsnips 149–51

pasta

bell pepper & tomato orzo soup
202–3

creamy spiced sausage 198–9

harissa & tahini lamb spaghetti
200–1

mushroom spaghetti, pistachio
& garlic 208–9

orzo, bean & herb salad 42

pistachio pesto salad 26–7

samosa 212–13

spiced eggplant & tomato
spaghetti 214–15

see also noodles

patties, feta & bean 82–3

peanut butter 173, 204

pearl barley, soup e jow 211

peas 73, 125, 212–13

black-eyed 42–3

yellow split 111

pesto, pistachio 26

pie

root vegetable 149–51

pine nuts 10, 53, 57

pistachios 18, 26, 107, 149, 208,
226, 228

pitta bread 70, 74, 86, 158

polow

Afghani 191–3

baghala, & lamb shanks 188–90

cheat's zereshk 194–5

pomegranate

feta & bean patties 82

ras el hanout sweet potatoes 165

in salads 12–13, 30, 37, 46

pomegranate molasses 13, 17, 30,
82, 100, 174, 185

potatoes

& cheese puffs 54–5

curried potato salad 38–9

with ras el hanout & lamb rib
chops 109

roast, with tomato, bell pepper
& harissa sauce 166–7

with spinach & eggs, fried
168–9

taas kabab 121

tavuk güveç 128–9

puff pastry 53, 54, 57

Q

quince jelly 118

R

ras el hanout 15, 109, 118–19

raspberry & pistachio crêpe cake
228–9

rice

Afghani polow 191–3

baghala polow & lamb shanks 189

black, broccolini & harissa salad
40–1

black, & butternut salad 30–1

cabbage "bowl" dolma 147

cheat's zereshk polow 194–5

dampokhtak 196–7

mushroom salad 29

Persian dolmeh e barg 111

spiced & soupy seafood 134–5

tahchin 125

ricotta salad 44–6

S

salmon, & barberry butter 132–3

sausage pasta 198–9

seafood, spiced & soupy rice 134–5

sesame seeds 86, 200, 204

shortbread, tea, cranberry, orange
& macadamia cookies 234–5

shrimp

spiced & soupy seafood 134–5

spicy fritters 78–9

tamarind vermicelli, orange &
pomegranate salad 46–7

soup

bell pepper, tomato & pasta
202–3

soup e jow 210–11

spinach 168–9

stews

chicken tagine 90–1

kid's chicken korma 130–1

lamb & potato 114–15

lamb tagine 96–7

spiced coconut chicken 206–7

taas kabab 120–1

tavuk güveç 128–9

strawberry cups 222–3

sumac 62, 149, 177

sweet potato 86–7, 164–5

T

taas kabab 120–1

tagine

chicken 90–1

lamb 96–7

tahchin 125–7

tahini

almond & chocolate cookies
232–3

garlic yogurt 123

& harissa lamb spaghetti 200–1

"hummus" salad 22

Mama Ghanoush 158–9

& pistachio sauce 208

spiced, with eggplant 170–1

yogurt with sweet potatoes 165

tamarind 46, 64–5, 153

tarts

zucchini 52–3

tavuk güveç 128–9

tea, shortbread cookies 234–5

tomatoes

bean, bell pepper & thyme
khorak 141

bell pepper & harissa sauce 166

& bell pepper pasta soup 202–3

cabbage "bowl" dolma 147

chicken shawarma salad 14

dream platter 20–1

& eggplant pasta 214–15

& feta fritters 180–1

halloumi & avocado wraps 85

halloumi skewers 162

nimroo mirzai 160–1

& pomegranate eggplants 185

roast, with labneh & sumac
spice oil 176–7

roasted vegetable & labneh
tartines 81

in sabich 74

semi-dried 10, 26, 34, 41, 141

spiced sausage pasta 198–9

spiced & soupy seafood 134–5

sublime BHT 70–1

taas kabab 121

tavuk güveç 128–9

tuna & bean salad 34–5

vegetable layers, baked 138–9

torsh e shami 116–17

tortillas 66–7, 85

tuna, tomato & bean salad 34–5

turmeric 99, 121, 178

V

vermicelli, shrimp salad 46–7

vine leaves 111

W

walnuts 45

watermelon salad 44–6

Y

yogurt

with charred broccoli 154

feta & lemon 145

garlic & oregano 181

harissa 66, 86

Mama Ghanoush 158–9

potato, spinach & eggs, fried
169

with roasted tomatoes 177

roasted vegetable tartines 81

in tahchin 125

tahini 123, 165

turmeric-spiced 178–9

Z

za'tar 69, 81

zucchini

lemon, feta & pine nut tart 53

with lemon & feta yogurt 144–5

roasted vegetable & bean salad
32–3

vegetable layers, baked 138–9

Acknowledgments

A big thank you to Octopus Publishing for always supporting me and allowing me to take my books and recipes in a direction I like. Thank you to my publisher Stephanie Jackson for guiding me each time, and to Sybella Stephens for translating "Sabrina gobbledygook" into English with great aplomb. To the brilliant and BEST publicity team any author could wish for, Publicity & Marketing Director Caroline Brown and her razor-sharp team Megan, Matt, Karen, Victoria, Hazel, Charlotte, Rosa, and Ed, thank you for all you do before and after publication. Another huge thank you to Jaz Bahra, Jonathan Christie, and Peter Hunt for consistently creating intricate and beautiful books, inside and out. I know it gets harder each time, but you always deliver and I'm so grateful. Thank you also to Kevin Hawkins for all you have done, and to Anna Bond for all your support and kindness.

To one of the world's most patient and kind human beings, Kris Kirkham, you really are the very best photographer a girl could ask for. Beyond that, you are always my brother and friend and I am thrilled and surprised that you are able to conjure up such stunning and different photographs every single time. Thanks to Phoebe and Rob for all the laughs, cuddles, and Yorkshire tea!

To my brilliant and incredibly gifted food stylist Laura Field for creating the beautiful food and styling of my recipes, along with Lizzie Evans, who kindly did some food styling as well as being part of the world's best (and most tolerant) team of brilliant home economists. Thank you to Sarah and Hilary for also doing such a great job and for being so careful with my cherished and extra-special Persian recipes, and for understanding they had to look and be perfect.

To Agathe for choosing and supplying the perfect props and crockery for this book, as always, and to baby Lily who brought endless joy to our shoots with her smiles, giggles, and love for my roast lamb.

Thank you to Richard and Trish Sinclair for the best and only venue I like to shoot at, The Warehouse studio—very much a home away from home; you are like family to me.

To my agent Martine Carter who, by now, should have received some kind of Nobel prize for her patience in guiding me in my career, thank you for your solid support and endless pep talks over the last 11 years. You remain the longest relationship I've ever had, and I'm so fortunate to have your no-nonsense, tough love in my life. Thank you for being a dear friend as well as the best agent a girl could ask for.

Lastly, thank you to my husband, who eats everything I cook, whether he likes it or not, and praises it to the heavens every time. Thanks to Mama G, my faithful assistant and Mother, who has still never cooked me a meal (except for that one incident of spaghetti in the 1980s that involved you emptying a whole jar of ground pepper into the sauce!). And to the kids, Connor and Olly, who now, thankfully, love everything I cook.